Nicholson's

Guide

Over six hundred
selected places to eat to suit
all tastes and pockets

ROBERT NICHOLSON PUBLICATIONS

GEOGRAPHIA

ISBN 0 905522 10 9

© Robert Nicholson Publications Limited
24 Highbury Crescent
London, N5 1RX.

First published 1975
2nd edition 1977
3rd edition 1978
4th edition 1980

London Map
© Robert Nicholson Publications Limited
based upon the Ordnance Survey
with the sanction of the Controller of
Her Majesty's Stationery Office.
Crown Copyright reserved.
London Underground map by kind
permission of London Transport

All other maps
© Robert Nicholson Publications Limited

Great care has been taken throughout this book
to be accurate but the publishers cannot accept
responsibility for any errors which appear.

Typeset by Dolphin Fototype Ltd, Aylesbury, Bucks
Printed by E. T. Heron, Silver End, Witham, Essex

Contents

Introduction

Over 600 good restaurants are divided into categories
to make it easy to find exactly what you want. There is
of course ample provision for those with classical
tastes—but if you feel a little adventurous, try some
Lebanese, Polynesian or Thai cooking for the first time.
A warm summer evening creates the perfect mood for
eating outdoors or by the riverside, while the simple,
informal atmosphere of a wine bar will help you to relax
with a friend. There are even restaurants for people as
concerned about their health as their taste-buds. Add
restaurants which keep you entertained and those
which cater for people who want good food without
spending a fortune—and you have a comprehensive
guide to the best eating in London.

Symbols and abbreviations

L—Lunch
D—Dinner
Open to 23.30—Last orders or they actually
  close then
(Reserve)—Advisable to reserve
(M)—Membership required

Average cost of a meal for one inclusive of VAT
  but without wine:
£   —£5.00 and under
££   —£10.00 and under
£££   —Under £15.00
£££+ —Over £15.00

Credit cards
A — Access (incorporating MasterCard, Eurocard)
Ax— American Express
B — Barclaycard (incorporating Visa)
Cb— Carte blanche
Dc— Diners club

African

The Calabash   6 J 23
38 King St WC1. 01-836 1973. African cooking in the basement of the very modern Africa Centre in Covent Garden. A comfortable room with a bar and easy chairs at one end. Masks and head-dresses on the walls. Interesting, tasty selection of dishes: beef with green bananas and coconut cream, chicken ground nut stew, beef stew, blackeyed beans, grey mullet. North African wine available. *LD open to 22.30. Closed Sun.* Ax.B.Dc. **££.**

American

American food invaded London in a big way a few years ago and was an instant success. Mainly hamburgers with various dressings and relishes; the taste caught on and spread rapidly across the city. This section shows the variety in location and type of the various hamburger joints in London. Also see 'Inexpensive Eating.' For carveries, English roast and grill rooms see the 'English' section.

Joe Allen   6 K 23
13 Exeter St WC2. 01-836 0651. Opened without fanfare in a converted warehouse in Covent Garden, the London 'Joe Allen' follows the pattern of the New

York and Paris restaurants. First-rate cocktail bar; blackboard menu of steaks, hamburgers, delicious spinach salad, spare ribs and chilli followed by cheese-cake or pecan pie. A fashionable place. Very crowded every night, especially after the theatre. *LD (Reserve) open to 01.00.* **££.**

American Haven   2 H 19
70–71 New Bond St W1. 01-352 7182.
291 Finchley Rd NW3. 01-794 5707.
Both share the same basic hamburger menu, with eight sorts of hamburgers in different weights and sizes. Also chicken in a basket, steak, chilli con carne. The Bond St branch is the most fun, with photos of Chaplin, Laurel and Hardy, and a continuous run of old silent comic shorts. *LD open to 24.00.* **£.**

Brooke's   1 I 8
68 Old Brompton Rd SW7. 01-584 8993. Large and colourful room on street level. More intimate eating downstairs. A varied menu where pies, quiches and other savouries vie with many delicious versions of hamburger. Elaborate sweets as well as traditional bread and butter pudding. *LD open to 00.30.* Ax.B. **£.**

Bunters   6 J 25
109 Kingsway WC2. 01-242 5426. Abounding with Billy Bunter memorabilia—caps, ties, blown-up Annual pictures. Street level dining area is self-service at lunchtime and offers kebabs, spare ribs, salads, in addition to a variety of hamburgers. Waitress service in the evenings. Downstairs, in a cosier atmosphere, a more sophisticated French cuisine menu is available for luncheon only. *LD open to 01.00. Closed Sun, L Sat.* A.Ax.B.Dc. **£.**

Burger King   5 J 21
25 Coventry St W1. 01-930 5661. First of a popular American hamburger chain opened in this country. Handy for a late night snack or take away. Quick and efficient service. The motto is 'have it your way'—hamburgers will be cooked to your specification, with your choice of trimmings. *LD open to 01.00. Fri & Sat to 02.00.* **£.**

Chicago Pizza Pie Factory   5 J 19
17 Hanover Sq W1. 01-629 2669. Crowded American

restaurant, paraphernalia brought from Chicago cover the walls, everything from street signs to old movie posters. Tapes of the local Chicago radio station are flown in weekly. Serves 'big-shouldered' pizzas which are cooked in deep pans—more filling is used than the average British pizza. The speciality is hand-made sausage and cheese served with different herbs. For dessert American cheesecake, carrot cake or ice-cream. *LD open to 23.30. Closed Sun.* **£.**

Drones   **5 J** 12
1 Pont St SW1. 01-235 9638. Stylish decor as befits its address. Spread over two floors, with plain white walls, plenty of foliage and unusual stained glass windows. Packed with young customers. Basic hamburgers, salads, shakes and ices plus more ambitious dishes. *LD open to 24.00.* A.Ax.B.Dc. **££.**

Great American Disaster   **4 K** 6
335 Fulham Rd SW10. 01-351 1188. The first and most steadily popular of all hamburger joints, whose arrival unleashed a shoal of eager imitators. A bar, pounding rock music and usually very long queues outside as no reservations are accepted. Great hamburgers, chicken, Texas chilli, spare ribs; all accompaniments provided: iced water, salads and relishes. *LD open to 24.00. Fri & Sat to 01.00.* **£.**

Great American Disaster   **2 I** 12
9 Beauchamp Place SW3. 01-589 0992. Popular, crowded cousin of the first ever London hamburger place. Loud rock music, blow-ups of US catastrophies induce a cheerful 'eat, drink and be merry' philosophy. Eating in elevated wooden booths along one side of the narrow room. Salads, all sorts of weights and variety of hamburgers, steaks and grills. Efficient service. *LD open to 24.00. Fri & Sat to 01.00.* **£.**

L. S. Grunt's Chicago Pizza Pie Factory   **6 J** 23
12 Maiden Lane WC2. 01-379 7722. Lively pizza hideout in converted electricity sub-station. Large mural of Chicago by night and day, lit up by flashing lights and a cloud projector. Serve-yourself American salad bar concocted from a Victorian bath-tub. Superior deep dish pizzas 'wittily' entitled, 'Some Like

It Hot', 'Memories Are Made of This', 'Yes Sir, She's My Baby', and the 'Great Grunter'. Special chocolate cheesecake to follow. Polynesian cocktails. Also take-aways and ready-to-freeze pizza portions. *LD open to 23.30. Closed Sun.* £.

Hamburger Heaven   2 C 15
212 Edgware Rd W2. 01-723 2009. Crowded Western-style hamburger joint. Pictures of famous boxers on the wall. Not very good for a tête à tête as rock music is played very loudly. Typical selection of hamburgers. Some tables outside in summer months. *LD open to 24.00.* £.

Hard Rock Café   2 I 16
150 Old Park Lane W1. 01-629 0382. Fashionable hamburger joint, just off Hyde Park Corner. Vast room on two levels with a shorts bar and colour TV at one end. Large ceiling fans and pool lamps, huge wooden tables and non-stop blaring rock music. The hamburgers and steaks are excellent—all prime meat. Other favourites are grilled cheese, bacon, tomato and lettuce sandwiches, shakes, sodas and elaborate desserts. Expect a very long queue outside or have a drink at the bar while you wait. *LD open to 00.30.* £.

McDonald's
Branches all over London. Sit down and enjoy their famous swift service and efficient, clean, modern surroundings. Also take-away. Average hamburgers and chips; delicious thick milkshakes. Good value.

Most are open for LD to 23.00. **£.**
Following are but a selection:

57 Haymarket SW1. 01-930 9302.	**5 J** 21
108 Kensington High St W8. 01-937 3705.	**1 D** 5
1–4 Marble Arch W2. 01-402 6297.	**2 E** 16
8–10 Oxford St W1. 01-580 7213.	**2 G** 21
37 The Strand WC1. 01-839 6086.	**6 K** 23
155 Victoria St SW1. 01-828 6911.	**5 M** 17

Maxwells
76 Heath St NW3. 01-794 5450. Eat bistro-style in a relaxed multi-level room. Of course, various hamburgers, but also steaks and kebabs; many crunchy salads with a Hawaiian touch. Rich sweets. Separate bar, games room and garden for outdoor eating in the summer. *LD open to 00.30.* **£.**

Parsons 4 K 8
311 Fulham Rd SW10. 01-352 0651. American café with informal waiters and shared tables. Urbane interior—plenty of rubber plants, mirrors and cool beige walls. Trendy clientele. Large portions of spaghetti (second helping free), cauliflower cheese, leek oven dishes, steaks and good hamburgers. Taped rock music. *LD open to 01.00.* **£.**

Peppermint Park 5 J 22
13–14 Upper St Martins Lane WC2. 01-836 5234. Crowded, lively atmosphere in this brightly decorated restaurant. Predominantly green with splashes of vivid pink. There is a cocktail bar. Taped music only. American food: steak sandwiches, hot dogs, hamburgers, salt beef with fresh salads. *LD (Reserve) open to 02.00. Sun to 24.00.* **££.**

Prohibition 2 I 22
43 Old Compton St W1. 01-437 0763. Central, friendly hamburger haven. Glass pictures on the walls and etched windows. Plenty of hamburger choice widened by southern fried chicken and spare ribs. All-American desserts. Unlicensed. *LD open to 24.00.* **£.**

Rock Garden 6 J 23
6/7 The Piazza, Covent Garden WC2. 01-240 3961. Restaurant upstairs and on street level—tables outside

in the summer (no need to worry about showery weather as it is covered). Music, casual service and cocktail bar. Hamburgers, spare ribs, house specialities; delicious devil's food cake to follow. Live concerts downstairs in a converted vegetable warehouse. Breakfast served. *LD open to 24.00. Closed Sun.* **£.**

Roxy Diner 3 E 32

297 Upper St N1. 01-359 3914. Small, fresh room, sparsely decorated with hanging plants and two-tone green walls. Basic hamburger fare with some good salads, scampi, Mexican chilli. Weight conscious customers should try the vegetarian salad. Friendly service. Traditional Sunday lunch. *LD open to 24.00.* **£.**

Sloane's Café 2 I 14

116 Knightsbridge SW1. 01-589 6873. Not exactly Sloane Ranger territory. A sophisticated hamburger joint with mustard colour walls, paintings and two great fireplaces. Hamburgers, steaks and salads; a wide variety of lagers. Choice of over 30 cocktails from the bar. Late night licence. *LD (Reserve D) open to 03.00. Sun to 24.00.* A.Ax.B.Dc. **£.**

Sour Grapes Café 1 I 11

93 Old Brompton Rd SW7. 01-584 9002. Pleasant airy café with plenty of variety in both hamburgers, grills (from charcoal or wood) or salads and quiches. Daily changes in choice of main dishes. Tables on the patio in summer: inside cane tables and chairs, art déco wallpaper and a ceiling hung with fans. Lager, wine and generous portions. Very popular. *LD open to 01.00.* **£.**

Widow Applebaum's Deli & Bagel Academy 2 F 19

46 South Molton St W1. 01-629 4649. American-Jewish delicatessen with a lengthy menu offering 101 dishes. Chopped liver, matzo balls, good hot pastrami, and a large selection of sandwiches, salads, burgers, ice-cream sodas and home-made apple strudel. Mirrors and period photos of New York in the jazz age. *LD open to 22.30. Closed Sun.* **£.**

Wolfe's Restaurant 2 G 16

34 Park Lane W1. 01-499 6897. Upstairs—downstairs hamburger restaurant with soft lighting, comfortable seating and quiet background music. Better selection of

regular main courses than is customary, including a Supersalad platter for the weight watcher or vegetarian. For dessert—waffles, yoghurt cups, cheesecake and a very rich American pecan pie. Milk shakes or cocktails, wine and beer. *LD open to 24.00.* A.Ax.B.Dc. **£.**

Chinese: General

Rice is the basis of all Chinese dishes. Minute quantities of vegetables, meat and fish are chopped to wafer-thin proportions and served as side dishes. The various side dishes should be eaten together so that the flavours combine. Nearly all these ingredients are steamed or fried with vegetable or peanut oil. 'Stir-frying' for only a few minutes is the technique. Vegetables such as lettuce and bean shoots can be delicious prepared in this way. Sauces also play an important part. Soy sauce is often used; many other foods are dipped into mustard or plum sauce. Especially good are the Chinese 'dim sum'—steamed savouries in bamboo baskets.

Chinese: Cantonese

The cooking of Canton and Southern China differs from Pekinese mainly by being more liquid. It is steamed, boiled or braised—herbs and sauces are widely used. A Chinese meal is intended as a communal experience and is best shared by about six people, all choosing different dishes. Delicately scented tea draws out the understated flavours. Gerrard Street in Soho is London's 'Chinatown'.

Canton   **2 I** 22
11 Newport Place WC2. 01-437 6220. Small but recently redecorated, the cooking here is strictly authentic. Home-made noodles, fried rice sticks with shrimps and pork, water-chestnut cake any time of the day or night. *LD open 24 hrs a day.* A.Ax.B.Cb.Dc. **£.**

Chuen Cheng Ku   **2 I** 21

17 Wardour St W1. 01-437 1398. Large complex of
restaurants, well patronised by Chinese customers.
Totally authentic food includes large portions of
delicious fish dishes: whole bass in ginger, shrimp chips,
bean curd soup. The dim sum are also recommended
with such dishes as marinated prawns wrapped in
paper, rice in lotus leaves and spare ribs. *LD (Reserve
D) open to 23.45.* **£.**

Far East   **2 I** 22

13 Gerrard St W1. 01-437 6148. Welcoming ship-
shape restaurant with very good lobster dishes. Either
choose a whole lobster or the fixed price lobster meal of
nine dishes. Also mouth-watering: bean curd with crab,
squid in ginger and soy bean sauce, black bean sauce
crab. *D open to 05.00.* **£.**

Good Friends

139 Salmon Lane E14. 01-987 5498. Large, simple
restaurant in London's East End. Renowned for good,
reliable cooking so booking is advisable. Crab, spring-
rolls, various soups and stuffed chicken are some of the
best dishes. Unlicensed so bring your own wine. *LD
(Reserve) open to 24.00.* A.Ax.B.Dc. **£.**

The Green Cottage

9 New College Parade, Finchley Rd NW3. 01-722
5305. Authentic Cantonese cooking up to Gerrard
Street proficiency. Pork, duck and spare ribs are
barbecued in the window. Deep fried wun-tun with
sweet and sour sauce, steamed sea bass with plum
sauce. Io-han vegetables. Welcoming service. *LD open
to 23.00.* **£.**

Han's of Chelsea   **4 L** 6

7 Park Walk SW10. 01-352 3546. Acclaimed and
congenial newcomer to the Cantonese scene. Quiet,
tasteful decor with light background music. For
starters, Han's special hors d'oeuvres (seaweed, crispy
chicken, sweet and sour pork, spiced meat cutlets, crab
meat balls, sesame prawn fingers, crab fried with egg).
To follow: stuffed duck, steamed sea bass with plums,
pan fried prawns in oyster sauce. Also authentic
Malaysian Chinese menu. *LD open to 24.00. Closed
Sun.* A.Ax.B.Cb.Dc. **££.**

Kam Tong   **1 B** 10
59 Queensway W2. 01-229 6065. A useful, not over-
expensive, lively restaurant just north of Hyde Park,
and close to Queens Ice Skating Rink. Enormous
variety of dim sum at lunchtime and pastries stamped
with Chinese characters, stuffed with chicken or garlic
paste. *LD open to 23.30.* **£.**

Lee Ho Fook   **2 I** 22
15 Gerrard St W1. 01-734 9578. Much loved by
Chinese and usually crowded. Eat in cave-like rooms
with carved ceilings. Excellent cooking with generous
portions at reasonable prices. Service is slow, so don't
be in a hurry. Try the shrimps in black bean sauce, duck
stew with abalone, lobster, sliced steak in black bean
sauce, suckling pig. Famous for its dim sum (steamed
savouries in bamboo baskets). *LD open to 23.30.* **£.**

Lee Ho Fook   **2 I** 22
4 Macclesfield St W1. 01-437 3474. *The* place for a
'quickie'. Well cooked dishes of roast pork or duck,
bamboo shoots and shrimps brought swiftly. Or just
have a large bowl of steaming oriental broth. Good
value if in a hurry. *LD open to 21.00.* **£.**

Lido   **2 I** 22
41 Gerrard St W1. 01-437 4431. Large, bustling
restaurant on three floors in the heart of the Chinese
quarter in Soho which serves meals into the small
hours. Special dishes section is printed in Chinese.
Known for their substantial noodle soups, baked crab
and ginger, crispy pork and chicken with cashew nuts.
D open to 04.30. A.Ax.B.Dc. **£.**

Loon Fung   **2 I** 22
37 Gerrard St W1. 01-437 5429. Sophisticated decor in
which to enjoy the companionship of Chinese families
eating dim sum from the large choice on display. Dim
sum available *to 18.00 only.* Black bean chicken and
fish ball soup also available. If you liked the food, you
could try it yourself with the ingredients from the
Chinese supermarket next door. *LD (Reserve) open to
23.15.* **£.**

Lotus House   **2 D** 16
61–69 Edgware Rd W2. 01-262 4341. Reliable

Cantonese food in comfortable Chinese surroundings. Nightly pianist. Try the batter-fried prawns and lemon chicken. *LD open to 01.00.* A.Ax.B.Cb.Dc. **££.**

Marco Polo   **4 L 11**
95 King's Rd SW3. 01-352 0306. A smart, attractive restaurant with a large Cantonese menu. Some specialities include fish in ginger and soy sauce, Cheng Yan Chicken. *LD open to 24.00.* A.Ax.B.Dc. **£.**

Pang's
215 Sutherland Avenue W9. 01-289 0970. The second branch in the Pang group. Predominantly Cantonese food served in sophisticated surroundings. Delightful trellis work screens and a waterfall by the front door. Try braised lobster with spring onion and ginger, teppan beef, or the specially prepared Cantonese version of Peking duck. Party rooms available but banquets must be ordered in advance. *LD open to 23.00. Closed Mon.* A.Ax.B.Dc. **££.**

Poons   **6 J 23**
41 King St WC2. 01-240 1743. A more ambitious derivative of the Poons in Lisle Street. Pleasantly modern decor, cocktail bar. Tables are grouped around a glassed-in kitchen area; the ceaseless activity of the chefs provides constant diversion. The menu makes fascinating reading with its list of some 350 dishes. Special sections of eel and pigeon dishes, and of course the Poons' speciality of wind-dried meats, pork belly, duck and duck liver sausage. These perhaps are an acquired taste, but other dishes, crab, Beggar's chicken, steamed fish with ginger, are sure to please. *LD (Reserve D) open to 23.30. Closed Sun.* Ax.Dc. **££.**

Shangri La   **2 I 12**
233 Brompton Rd SW3. 01-584 3658. A snackbar with plenty of cheap meals such as chop suey and curried prawns. Downstairs for a sophisticated, candle-lit restaurant serving good crispy fried prawns. Speedy, obliging service. *LD open to 23.30. Closed L Sun.* A.Ax.B.Dc. **££.**

Uncle Pang
30 Temple Fortune Parade, Finchley Rd NW11. 01-455 9444. Fairly chic suburban restaurant offering a most satisfying selection of popular Cantonese dishes.

Some favourite specialities are: deep-fried duck with minced prawn, braised stuffed bean curd, fried rice noodle Singapore-style and spicy chicken roll. Attentive service. *LD open to 23.00.* Ax.B.Dc. **££.**

Wong Kei   **2 I** 21
Rupert Court, Rupert St W1. 01-437 3071. Tucked away down a small alley, a genuine restaurant packed out at lunchtime. Set noodle base dishes or the à la carte menu which includes unusual specialities: braised duckweb, as well as sweet and sour pork and chicken with beans. *LD open to 02.00.* **£.**

Zen (Chelsea)

Chinese: Pekinese

The dishes of Peking, Formosa and Northern China are considered to be the highest form of Chinese cuisine and often equal in quality to the best French cooking. The food is drier and sharper than Cantonese (often roasted or quick fried) and the seven or eight courses are all eaten separately as a 'banquet'—a leisurely ceremonial occasion ideally shared between four and six people. If possible, order the day before—you can leave the choice to the restaurant. The great dishes are Peking duck and Mongolian hot-pot.

Chelsea Rendezvous   **4 K** 9
4 Sydney St SW3. 01-352 9519. Smoothly sophisticated restaurant. The food is of a very high standard and derived from Pekinese and Shanghai cooking. Many devoted regulars. Especially good fish, mixed vegetables and Peking duck. *LD open to 24.00.* Ax.B.Cb.Dc. **££.**

Chiu Chow Inn   **2 I** 22
21 Lisle St WC2. 01-437 6419. Simple, three-floor restaurant in the heart of Chinatown. Good choice of Peking specialities and fish in unusual sauces: squid with black bean and pepper sauce, sea bass with soy and ginger, sliced fish fillets in wine sauce, roast Peking duck, shredded smoked chicken with yellow bean sauce. Saké lavishly poured. *LD open to 23.30.* A.B.Dc. **£.**

Dumpling Inn   **2 I** 22
15a Gerrard St W1. 01-437 2567. Lively, crowded,
rather confined Soho restaurant. Mr Wong, the chef,
excels with his pork dumplings, prawns in chilli sauce,
fried seaweed and beef in oyster sauce. *LD open to
23.30.* Ax.B.Dc. **££.**

Gallery Rendezvous   **2 H** 20
53 Beak St W1. 01-734 0445. Dine in opulence in a
Chinatown banqueting suite or among one of the best
collections of original Chinese paintings in London. A
highly successful 'Rendezvous chain' enterprise where
the food matches the high standard of its surroundings.
A choice of banquets or order specialities ahead. Snow
prawn balls, barbecued Peking duck, exceptional spare
ribs and stuffed pancakes. *LD (Reserve) open to 23.00.*
Ax.Dc. **££.**

Great Shanghai   **2 H** 22
42 Dean St W1. 01-437 9455. One of London's first
Shanghai restaurants. Unusual and tasty dishes include
fish soup Shanghai, pancakes with pork and spring
onions and rice dumplings in wine and rice soup. *LD
open to 23.00.* A.Ax.B.Dc. **£.**

Hung Foo
6–8 West Hill, Wandsworth SW18. 01-870 0177. A
family-run restaurant in recently extended and
redecorated premises. Friendly and authentic with its
tables laid with finger bowls and chopsticks, soft
Chinese music and its long list of Peking specialities.
Grilled Peking chicken, sizzling lamb cooked at the
table, prawn toast with sesame seeds, toffee coated
apples and bananas. *LD (Reserve D) open to 24.00.
Closed Sun.* **£.**

Kuo Yuan
217 High Rd, Willesden NW10. 01-459 2297. Despite
modest surroundings in a local high street, this busy
restaurant serves some excellently prepared, authentic
Pekinese food. The set menus are particularly good
value: hot and sour soup, Chinese dumplings, crispy
aromatic Peking duck, sweet and sour pork on crispy
rice, chicken and almond in bean sauce, spare ribs,
prawns in chilli and crunchy fried seasonal vegetables.
Quick service. *L Sat & Sun only. D (Reserve Sat) open
to 23.00.* **££.**

Lee Yuan   1 E 5

40 Earls Court Rd W8. 01-937 7047. Small and unsmart, but with first-class Peking cooking. Also some of the better Szechuan dishes. Specialities are toasted prawns and Peking duck (best order in advance). Chinese wine to drink. *LD (Reserve D) open to 23.45.* A.Ax.B.Cb.Dc. **£.**

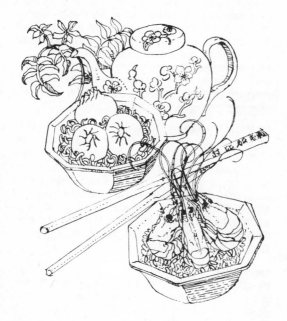

Mandarin

297c Finchley Rd NW3. 01-794 6119. Increasingly popular, even though 'out of the way'. No pretensions to grandeur, but a friendly 'local' atmosphere. Some unusually good dishes; crispy duck pancakes, stir fried squid with Chinese vegetables, seaweed salad. The highlight is the nine course Peking banquet which must be ordered in advance. *LD (Reserve) open to 23.30. Closed L Sun.* **£.**

Mandarin Duck

12 Sutton Parade, Church Rd, Hendon NW4. 01-203 4064. Szechuan food from South West China, hotter and spicier than in other Chinese restaurants with the liberal use of chilli and peppers, is served here. Enjoy prawns or crispy beef with chilli sauce, pepper soup or dumplings in this garishly decorated restaurant. Convivial ambience. *LD open to 24.00.* A.Ax.B.Dc. **£.**

Mr Chow   2 I 13

151 Knightsbridge SW1. 01-589 7347. Here is a place to be seen and to see who's there. Worth it also for the modern decor and contemporary paintings by Dine, Richard Smith and Patrick Caulfield. Make no mistake, this is a lordly eating house with a young staff and a host who smiles genuinely while he brings the glazed duck. Essential for introduction to Chinese eating as practised in SW1. Peking duck, sole in wine. *LD (Reserve) open to 23.45.* A.Ax.B.Cb.Dc. **££.**

Mr Kai of Mayfair   2 G 17

65 South Audley St W1. 01-493 8988. Modern, stylish restaurant in non-Chinese eating territory. Simple decor, plants and a mock blossom tree bearing flowers of silk on each of the two floors. Good crispy Peking duck, sizzling lamb, chilli prawn in fresh pineapple and chilli beef in bird's nest. Legendary touch to the names of several specialities. Efficient waiters and charming Chinese ladies serving drinks. *LD (Reserve D) open to 23.30.* A.Ax.B.Cb.Dc. **££.**

Paper Tiger   1 H 10

10–12 Exhibition Rd SW7. 01-584 3737. Intimate and fashionable basement restaurant providing a high standard of Szechuan and Pekinese cuisine. Spicy dumplings, curried Wan Tun, drunken fish in rice wine sauce, Bang Bang chicken and sesame prawn.toast are some of the more exotic dishes. *LD (Reserve D) open to 23.30.* A.Ax.B.Dc. **££.**

Peking

3 Westbourne Grove W2. 01-727 4328. Highly elaborate Chinese decor with a hand-cut ceiling displaying dragons, silk pictures on the walls and a superbly carved Chinese partition by the entrance. Reliable cooking in this well-established restaurant.

Typical Peking specialities: crispy duck, prawns in ginger and spring onion, as well as a more spicy sesame flavoured chicken. Attracts many overseas visitors. *LD open to 23.30.* A.Ax.B.Dc. **££.**

Richmond Rendezvous
1 Paradise Rd. 01-940 5114. Also at 1 Wakefield Rd. 01-940 0579. Part of the prolific 'Rendezvous chain', with yet another branch—the Kew Rendezvous at 110 Kew Rd. 01-948 4343. All decorated in a modern style and serving largely similar dishes. Choose from sliced sole in wine, toasted prawns, chicken and almonds or beef with chilli. Special Pekinese banquets can be ordered. Toffee coated apples to end the meal. *LD open to 23.30.* A.B.Ax.Dc. **£.**

Soho Rendezvous   2 I 22
21 Romilly St W1. 01-437 1486. Yet another branch of the 'Rendezvous chain', with properly and superbly cooked classic Peking dishes. The comfortable air-conditioned surroundings and the absence of chopsticks unless requested, are customs borrowed from the West. But it's Chinese at the kitchen stove, out of which come the delectable grilled stuffed dumplings, bean curd in batter, diced chicken in yellow bean sauce. *LD (Reserve) open to 23.45.* A.Ax.B.Dc. **££.**

Tung Hsing
22 North End Rd NW11. 01-458 1887. Some now famous chefs started out in this kitchen. It's not smart, but serves very good Peking banquets. Recommended are the sweet and sour pork, quick fried prawns with green pepper and sliced sole with Chinese wine sauce. *LD open to 23.30. Closed Mon.* Ax.Dc. **£.**

Welcome
68 Belsize Lane NW3. 01-794 9217. Much frequented by local clientele, this unassuming restaurant with its slightly shabby decor gives good value for money. Reservations are essential. Well worth sampling the set menus—finely prepared Peking duck, deep fried beef with chilli and tasty sliced chicken with lemon sauce. *LD open to 24.00.* Ax. **£.**

Dinner and dance

Do you want to dance? Or sit back and watch a spectacular? Or perhaps both? But above all, the food must be right? Then flick through this section; there's something for everyone. Don't be put off by the (*M*) Membership sign. Most clubs usually have guest membership arrangements; where not, we have mentioned it. There is often an entrance fee as well as membership to pay, but we have purposely included many dine and dance and theatre restaurants that do not insist on fees of this kind.

Annabel's   **2 H** 18
44 Berkeley Square W1. 01-629 2350. Well-known fashionable disco; like the members, the food is of a distinguished quality. One of the best short menus in London presided over by Louis (formerly manager of Mirabelle). Raspberries in December. Asparagus in January; the best truffles all year round. Exclusive and expensive. Overseas visitors should arrange for a member to fix entry in advance. *D open to 04.00. Closed Sun. (M).* **£££+.**

Bizzarro   **2 B** 12
18–22 Craven Rd W2. 01-723 6029. Wine, dine and dance in a lively Mediterranean atmosphere. Comprehensive Italian menu. Flamboyant service. Eating upstairs amidst alcoves and arches, dancing downstairs to a resident band. *LD (Reserve) open to 01.00. Closed Sun.* A.Ax.B.Dc. **£££.**

Boulogne   **2 I** 22
27 Gerrard St W1. 01-437 3186. Well-preserved nineteenth century rooms decorated with mirrors and Edwardian pieces. A standard range of French dishes adequately served. Traditional atmosphere. There is a resident quartet and a show with different dancers and singers every fortnight. An inclusive charge for those wanting dinner or an entrance fee for those just interested in using the bar. *D open to 02.30. Cabaret 23.00 & 01.00. Closed Sun.* A.Ax.B.Dc. **££.**

La Bussola
5 J 22

42–49 St Martin's Lane WC2. 01-240 1148. Cosy restaurant in the heart of theatreland, which still provides table d'hôte pre-theatre dinners. Two bands to dance to and an excellent Italian cuisine of consistently high standards: chicken cacciatore, fegato alla Veneziana. Also good antipasto and home-made soups. An elegant and relaxing dine and dance restaurant. *LD (Reserve) open to 01.30. Closed Sun, L Sat.* A.Ax.B.Dc. **£££+**.

Chanticleer
5 L 17

Roebuck House, Stag Place, Palace St SW1. 01-834 5695. Large but intimate Italian restaurant. Traditional English decor with roses always on the table. Try veal alla Martino, home-made pasta, avocado Chanticleer, scampi Cartoccio and filet of sole in Cinzano sauce. *Pianist Mon to Thur and dance to a three-piece band Fri and Sat. LD (Reserve) open to 24.00. Closed Sun, L Sat.* A.Ax.B.Dc. **££**.

Chaplins
2 I 20

9 Swallow St W1. 01-734 2649. Dark blue restaurant serving international cuisine—sole Colbert, scampi Pernod, liver Lyonnaise, various grills, caviar. Neat central dance floor with a resident quartet. Booking is absolutely essential. Smart clientele. *D (Reserve) open to 02.45. Cabaret 24.00. Closed Sun.* A.Ax.B.Cb.Dc. **£££+**.

The Click
4 L 4

533 King's Rd SW10. 01-352 7161. A newcomer to the dine and dance scene which has just recently opened on the premises of the previously popular and trendy Country Cousins venue. Under different management, the massive L-shaped room with its barn-like interior has been preserved and now carries a green and white colour scheme. A proper dance floor has been fitted, the bar has been extended and more tables and chairs have been added to accommodate the clientele. Simple English cuisine. Very informal and casual atmosphere. Dancing to a pianist, drummer and bassist. *D open to 24.00.* A.Ax.B.Dc. **£**.

Concordia Notte
2 B 12

29–31 Craven Rd W2. 01-723 3725. Sophisticated,

baroque dining room attracting la crème de la crème of society. Silver candlesticks, 17th century Sicilian-style paintings. Patronised by stars and even royalty. Haute cuisine Italian menu prepared by more than 10 chefs. Caviar, oysters, lobster. Special dishes like El Marinaro, shell fish mixed with veal, ham, beef, in white wine, garlic and tomatoes. Also Timbale Patrizia, strips of sole, scampi, lobster in brandy sauce. Excellent sweet trolley. Very spacious, studied service. Latin American cabaret, dancing to a band with Italian, English and Greek singers. Separate restaurant upstairs. *D (Reserve) open to 01.00. Cabaret and dancing to 02.00. Closed Sun.* A.Ax.B.Cb.Dc. **£££+**.

Elysée 2 G 22

13 Percy St W1. 01-636 4804. Lively, ethnic restaurant serving Greek food with some English and French dishes. Resident four-piece band and bouzouki music. Taverna atmosphere and plate breaking is encouraged. *LD (Reserve) open to 03.00. Cabaret 23.00 & 01.00.* A.Ax.B.Cb.Dc. **££**.

Los Espanoles 2 F 22

74 Charlotte St W1. 01-636 0036. Large Spanish-style restaurant. Carved ceiling, carpeted walls, Flamenco dancing. Continental cuisine emphasising Spanish dishes. Paella in different varieties, mixed seafood casserole, fresh sardines, baby pork. Spanish and English quartet. The acts occasionally vary but the atmosphere is always lively. *LD open to 02.30. Cabaret 24.00. Closed L Sat & Sun.* A.Ax.B.Dc. **££**.

Foobert's 2 G 20

Foubert's Place, Carnaby St. W1. 01-734 3630. Large, modern discotheque with plenty happening. Three bars, restaurant and snuggery. Informal and candle-lit, with occasional cabaret. English and American cooking— lamb chops, steaks, roast chicken, bacon and eggs, hamburgers. *LD open to 02.00. Closed L Sun, D Mon–Thur.* Ax.Dc. **£**.

L'Hirondelle 2 I 20

99 Regent St W1. 01-734 1511. Comfortable and pleasant, with air-conditioning, this theatre restaurant has two floor shows nightly, well-staged and flamboyant. Dancing to two groups *from 21.00.*

International menu in grand cuisine style: suprême de volaille Princesse, escalope de veau Hirondelle. A really spectacular evening out. *D (Reserve) open to 03.00. Closed Sun. Floorshows 23.00 & 01.30.* A.Ax.B.Cb.Dc. **£££.**

Legends   2 H 19

29 Old Burlington St W1. 01-437 9933. Light, airy, modern restaurant decorated with mirrors, plants and pictures of super-stars like Monroe, Clark Gable, James Dean and Humphrey Bogart. Well-prepared French cuisine. Glass frontage opens on sunny days to allow pavement eating. Trendy discotheque downstairs with a circular bar. Entrance fee only for non-diners. Brunch on Saturday and no dancing Sunday. *LD (Reserve) open to 02.00. Sun to 23.00.* A.Ax.B.Dc. **£££.**

New Georgian Club   2 G 19

4 Mills St W1. 01-629 2042. Club with cabaret twice nightly. Lounge bar with hostesses. Gourmet restaurant with international menu: escalope à la Georgian (breadcrumbed, with asparagus tips and cheese), shish kebab à la Turque. Their special châteaubriand is presented with six different vegetables. *D open to 01.30. Closed Sat & Sun. Cabaret 23.00 & 24.30. (M)* A.Ax.B.Cb.Dc. **£££.**

New Vintage Room   2 I 16

Inn on the Park, Hamilton Place W1. 01-499 0888. Sophisticated first floor restaurant decorated in royal blue and candle-lit. Three different menus at lunch. Inclusive à la carte menu in the evenings. International cuisine to a high standard. Dover sole, turbot, chicken Kiev, beef, duck. Resident band and singer. *LD (Reserve L) open to 24.00. Dancing to 02.00.* A.Ax.B.Cb.Dc. **£££+.**

Omar Khayyam   2 H 20

177 Regent St W1. 01-734 7675. Lavishly decorated in true Sultan's style. The 1001 nights' mood prevails, with opulent cabaret and authentic belly dancers. Both Turkish and Persian dishes on the menu: all sorts of shashlik, kebabs and very sweet sweets. Two bands to dance to and two floorshows nightly. *D (Reserve) open to 04.00. Closed Sun. Floorshows 22.00 & 01.00.* A.Ax.B.Cb.Dc. **£££.**

Quaglino's   5 J 19
16 Bury St SW1. 01-930 6767. Luxury, style and
glamour combined with consistently reliable cooking.
Very fashionable before the war, it still feels like a grand
Edwardian supper club. Sample a mixture of cooking
traditions including pinces de crabe Colbert, filet de
boeuf, escargots, steak tartare, grills and lamb's
kidneys in marsala. Set menu as well as à la carte
selections. Menu changes every three months. Nightly
cabaret and dancing. *LD (Reserve) open to 01.30.
Closed Sun, L Sat.* A.Ax.B.Cb.Dc. **£££+**.

Ronnie Scott's   2 H 22
47 Frith St W1. 01-439 0747. The best jazz in London
in a comfortable, often crowded-out atmosphere; subtle
lighting, but you can see the musicians. Ronnie Scott
habitually cracks loaded or far-fetched puns when
introducing the music, played by a succession of big-
name jazzmen, mostly USA imports. Friendly service.
Menu includes chicken dishes, steaks, pasta dishes and
salads. *D open to 03.00. Closed Sun. First set 22.30.
(M) not essential but entry depends on who is playing.*
A.Ax.B.Dc. **££**.

Roof Restaurant   2 I 16
Hilton Hotel, Park Lane W1. 01-493 8000. Dine 28
floors up for an intoxicating view over London. Tables
by the window are at a premium. Good dance floor and
two bands. Good French cooking; salade de homard
avec foie gras de canard, côte de veau en habite vert and
crêpes Suzette. *D open to 01.00. Closed Sun.*
A.Ax.B.Dc. **£££**.

Saddle Room Club   2 I 16
1a Hamilton Place W1. 01-499 4994. Popular intimate
disco. International clientele. Bistro in back with a
French menu that changes specialities regularly. *D
open to 04.00. Closed Sun. (M).* **££**.

Savoy Restaurant   6 K 23
Savoy Hotel, Strand WC2. 01-836 4343. Elegant,
formal and carrying a garden theme. Resident quartet
and dancing. World famous well-deserved reputation
for classic cooking and near perfect service: omelette
Brillat Savarin, boeuf in croûte François Villon,
goujonnettes de sole Imperial Palace. After theatre
suppers. *D open to 01.45. Closed Sun.* A.Ax.B. **£££**.

Stork Room 2 I 20
99 Regent St W1. 01-734 3686. Well-established club which maintains strong nostalgic associations with the late owner, Al Burnett (noted entertainer of the 50s). Twice nightly floorshow and singers. One band. English grill menu with steak and roast chicken. *D open to 04.00. Sun to 01.00. Floorshows 23.45 & 01.45. Sun. 24.00.* A.Ax.B.Cb.Dc. **££**.

Talk of the Town 2 I 22
Hippodrome Corner, Charing Cross Rd WC2. 01-734 5051. Theatre restaurant on a large and enormously popular scale. Biggest floorshow in London as well as international cabaret star solo show. Competent international menu with an extensive choice. Wide choice of rich sweets. Three bands; big nights Fri & Sat. *D open to 01.15. Closed Sun. Floorshow 21.30. Star cabaret 23.00.* A.Ax.B.Cb.Dc. **£££**.

Terrace Restaurant 2 H 16
Dorchester Hotel, Park Lane W1. 01-629 8888. Stately and gracious for an elegant dinner-dancing evening. Evening-coated waiters serve quality French cooking. Two bands. Noisette de veau à L'Esquire, sweetbreads, grouse and sole Dorchester. *D open to 01.00. Closed Sun, L Sat.* A.Ax.B.Cb.Dc. **£££**.

Tiberio 2 H 17
22 Queen St W1. 01-629 3561. Popular, crowded Italian late-night restaurant; show-biz clientele; exceptionally smooth and friendly service in this Italian rival to French grande cuisine. Excellent varied menu; food is beautifully presented: rack of lamb, osso buco, fettuccine alla panna, duck and quail. Dance till early morning to a quartet *from 23.00. D open to 01.00.* A.Ax.B.Cb.Dc. **£££**.

Tiddy Dol's 2 I 16
2 Hertford St W1. 01-499 2357/2358. An 18th century house in Shepherd Market, with a comfortable, intimate interior. Music room offers live music *till 23.00,* followed by dancing to the latest international sounds. Traditional English food includes excellent game dishes, cock-a-leekie soup, steak-and-kidney pie; good sherry trifle. *LD open to 02.00. Closed L Sat & Sun.* A.Ax.B.Cb.Dc. *Foreign currencies accepted.* **££**.

Le Trianon 2**I**13

Park Tower Hotel, Lowndes Square SW1. 01-235 8058. An unusually decorated dine and dance restaurant. Wide and varied menu with many worthy dishes in the classic French and English styles; fresh asparagus, beef from the trolley, filet Trianon, crêpes Suzette, soufflés. *LD open to 23.00. Trio plays from 20.30 exc. Mon.* A.Ax.B.Cb.Dc. **£££**.

La Valbonne 2 **H** 20

62 Kingly St W1. 01-439 7242. Popular disco that looks like a Carribean beach hut, adorned with mock foliage. Heart-shaped swimming pool for cooling off after a dance. Records and occasional live groups. Fine restaurant with international menu: beef Stroganoff and a wide choice of tempting sweets from the trolley. *D open to 03.00. Disco from 21.00. Closed Sun. (M) except for overseas or out of town visitors.* A.Ax.B.Cb.Dc. **££**.

English

'Real' English food is surprisingly difficult to get in England. The following restaurants are not coy about putting classic British dishes on the menu—such as kippers and smoked haddock; Yorkshire pudding; roast beef and real horseradish; toad-in-the-hole; Scotch porridge; Welsh rack of lamb; pease pudding and faggotts etc. We have listed what we consider the best and most authentic. Look out for fresh, wholesome meats and vegetables—it is the quality of the food and not the sauces that makes good English food. Also mentioned are a selection of 'carveries'. For the set price of a three course meal, customers can carve as much and as often as they like from enormous, succulent joints of beef, lamb and pork.

Aunties 2 **E** 22

126 Cleveland St W1. 01-387 3226. Simple, cheerful little restaurant, its decor vaguely Victorian, the walls hung with theatre bills. Straightforward wholesome cooking: home-made soups, Victoria pie, devilled rack of lamb, good fresh vegetables. Trifle, fruit fools, syllabub. *LD (Reserve) open to 21.30. Closed Sun, L Sat.* **£**.

Baker & Oven
2 C 19

10 Paddington St W1. 01-935 5072. The original ovens of the Victorian bakery are still in use here. Sound, simple food in generous quantity: pies, chops, roasts, game in season. Crowded, booking advisable. Half portions for children. *LD (Reserve) open to 23.00. Closed Sun, L Sat.* A.Ax.B.Dc. **££.**

Baron of Beef
6 M 30

Gutter Lane, Gresham St EC2. 01-606 6961. Vastly popular City restaurant. An expense account helps if your tastes stray towards the oysters or asparagus rather than more modest starters. Chief interest is in the roast beef and Yorkshire pudding from the trolley, beefsteak and kidney pie and roast duck with traditional accompaniments, lobster, sole and salmon; fresh vegetables, sometimes overcooked, pancakes or savouries, but no old-fashioned puddings. Fine wine list; notable claret served with due solemnity. *LD open to 22.00. Closed Sat & Sun.* A.Ax.B.Dc. **£££.**

Bulldog Chophouse
1 E 8

Royal Garden Hotel, Kensington High St W8. 01-937 8000. Lavishly fitted basement restaurant with a separate entrance from that of the hotel. The 'Olde Englishness' of the decor is a little at odds with the pianist playing Bacharach and the Beatles. Soups and fish, chops, steaks and grills, or roast beef from the

trolley of satisfactory quality and served in generous quantity. *LD open to 22.30. Closed L Sat.* A.Ax.B.Cb.Dc. **££.**

Bumbles 5 M 14
16 Buckingham Palace Rd SW1. 01-828 2903. Simple English cooking spiced with a sprinkling from abroad. The plain traditional dishes are the more successful; soups, steak and kidney pie, syllabubs. *LD (Reserve) open to 22.30. Closed Sun, L Sat.* A.Ax.B.Dc. **££.**

Carveries
All very good value, with a choice of simple starters and sweets included in the price. Carve as much and as often as you like from joints of beef, pork or lamb with a choice of vegetables. Pleasant informal atmosphere.

Kensington Close Hotel 1 E 7
Wright's Lane W8. 01-937 8170. *LD open to 22.30, 22.00 Sun. Closed L Sat.* A.Ax.B.Cb.Dc. **££.**

Kingsley Hotel 3 H 24
Bloomsbury Way WC1. 01-242 5881. *LD open to 21.00. Closed L Sat.* A.Ax.B.Cb.Dc. **££.**

Piccadilly Hotel 2 I 20
Piccadilly W1. 01-734 8000. *LD open to 21.30, 21.00 Sun.* A.Ax.B.Cb.Dc. **££.**

Rembrandt Hotel 1 I 10
Thurloe Place SW7. 01-589 8100. *LD open to 21.30.* A.Ax.B.Cb.Dc. **££.**

Tower Hotel 6 R 32
St Katherine's Way E1. 01-481 2575. Marvellously located carvery with a splendid view over St Katherine's Dock. *LD open to 22.00.* A.Ax.B.Cb.Dc. **££.**

Westmoreland Hotel
18 Lodge Rd, St John's Wood NW8. 01-722 7722. *LD open to 22.00.* A.Ax.B.Cb.Dc. **££.**

Connaught Rooms 3 I 24
Princes Restaurant, Gt Queen St WC2. 01-405 7811. Grandly decorated basement with appropriately formal service. Choose between the à la carte menu, mainly French, the cold table, or first-rate rib of beef and saddle of lamb from the trolley, with English cheeses and traditional puddings to follow. Popular place for

business lunches. Notable wine list. *L open to 14.30.*
Closed Sat & Sun. A.Ax.B.Dc. **££.**

Copper Grill 2 E 19
60 Wigmore St W1. 01-935 9803. Cosy downstairs
restaurant, its panelled walls hung with copper utensils
and ornaments. The set menu offers a wide choice, with
the emphasis on grills; steaks, chops and cutlets, fresh
salmon, trifle, cherry pie. A useful refuge for Oxford
Street shoppers. *LD open to 24.00.* Ax.B.Dc. **££.**

Drakes 4 K 9
2a Pond Place, Fulham Road SW3. 01-584 4555.
Smart but unpretentious split-level restaurant with old
country brick walls and floor, genuine Berkshire beams
and indoor fountain. Kitchen and revolving spit can be
seen from the well-designed dining area. Duck terrine
with hot herb bread, poached mackerel in white wine
and fennel, suckling pig, game, rack of lamb. Beef
Wellington is the house speciality. Try Bliss (pastry
stuffed with fresh raspberries and cream) or home-made
treacle tart for dessert. Bar upstairs. Fully air-
conditioned. *LD open to 23.00.* A.Ax.B.Dc. **££.**

English House 4 J 11
3 Milner St SW3. 01-584 3002. Charming dining room
in a private house. Antique chairs, expensive chintz wall
fabrics, brass base plates laid on quilted tablecloths and
cream table linen. That the menu consultant is an expert
on eighteenth century English food is reflected in the
imaginative, traditional dishes. Fish pie with scallops
and prawns, chicken mousse poached in cream,
Elizabethan sweet and savoury pork stew, excellent
steak and kidney pie. Genuine trifle, chocolate pie and
brown bread ice-cream. Specially selected wines. *LD*
(Reserve) open to 23.30. Closed Sun. A.Ax.B.Dc. **£££.**

Ebury Court Hotel 5 M 13
26 Ebury St SW1. 01-730 8147. A pretty alcoved room
in the depths of a charming old-fashioned hotel. Good
cooking, pleasant waitress service and the general
'English club' atmosphere explain the restaurant's
steady following. Salmon, trout, steak and kidney pie,
roasts and grills, and to follow, chocolate mousse,
lemon soufflé and sherry trifle. *LD (Reserve) open to*
21.00. **££.**

The Grange 6 J 23

39 King St WC2. 01-240 2939. Although large, a warm and intimate atmosphere pervades this elegant restaurant. Tastefully decorated in chocolate brown and beige with crisp white tablecloths. Food is predominantly English, choose from a selection of set menus. Pâtés, crudités, Shrewsbury lamb, beef Wellington; for dessert try their crème brûlée. Fully air-conditioned. *LD (Reserve) open to 23.30. Closed Sun, L Sat.* Ax. **££.**

Greenhouse 2 H 17

27a Hays Mews W1. 01-499 3331. Stark, white walls with lush green plants gives a light and summery effect. Service is efficient and friendly. For starters try cod's roe pâté with toast or creamy apple soup. Followed by roast rack of lamb with rosti potatoes, calves liver with apple and cranberries. For dessert lemon syllabub or chocolate brandy cream. Limited wine list. *LD (Reserve) open to 23.00. Closed Sun, L Sat.* A.Ax.B.Dc. **££.**

Guinea Grill Room 2 H 18

30 Bruton Place W1. 01-629 5613. Three rooms reached through a crowded Mayfair pub provide an unassuming setting for good plain cooking. The steaks and chops piled high beside the open grill are of obvious quality, and cooked to your order. With avocado or smoked fish to start, Stilton or strawberries to follow, you can do very well here, but bear in mind that the prices are not pub prices. *LD (Reserve) open to 22.45. Closed L Sat & Sun.* A.Ax.B.Cb.Dc. **£££+.**

Hathaways

13 Battersea Rise SW11. 01-228 3384. Simple furnishing with hessian walls and a Welsh dresser. Good fish and soups, guinea fowl with juniper, leek and ham tart, a variety of pies, traditional puddings, and a North American flavour in the chowders and ice-creams. Prompt, informal service. *D (Reserve) open to 22.30. Closed Sun.* A.Ax.B.Dc. **££.**

Hungry Horse 4 K 7

196 Fulham Rd SW10. 01-352 7757. Pleasant, unassuming restaurant with a standard range of English dishes. Cooking generally reliable; kedgeree,

straightforward roast beef and mutton, boiled beef and dumplings, steaks and chops, puddings and pies. Traditional sweets include treacle tart and Queen of puddings. Service is cheerful and bustling, booking advisable. *LD (Reserve) open to 24.00. Closed L Sun.* **££.**

Hunting Lodge 5 J 20

16 Lower Regent St SW1. 01-930 4222. A fun palace of the chase; elaborate decor in red and black, sporting guns, brass lamps, and a long and fancifully classified list of dishes, generally well prepared. Smoked fish, shellfish cocktails, pâtés and whitebait, a wide choice of soups. More substantial fish, roast beef, oxtail, loin of pork, lamb, duckling, chops and grills, cheese or a savoury to follow. Game in season on a separate menu. *LD open to 23.15. Closed Sun, L Sat.* A.Ax.B.Cb.Dc. **£££.**

Huntsman

15 Flask Walk, Hampstead NW3. 01-435 0769. Unusual country dishes prepared with imagination from good raw materials in modish cottage in one of the prettiest streets in Hampstead. Pies, jugged hare, fillet steak stuffed with oysters, pigeon pickled in walnuts and a variety of game. Not all the recipes are successful, but most are interesting to try. No licence, so you can afford to bring a good bottle. *D open to 23.00. Closed Sun.* A.B. **££.**

Lockets 5 O 18

Marsham Court, Marsham St SW1. 01-834 9552. Another of Mr Berkmann's restaurants, at the foot of a block of flats in the division bell area and doubtless frequented by many MPs. The 'Olde Englishe' dishes include 'lamb in the manner of Shrewsbury' which is served with a sauce fashioned with port, juniper and redcurrant jelly. 'Raspberry Lockets' consisting of fruit, cream and liqueur under a burnt sugar top is outstanding. Distinguished wine list. *LD open to 23.00. Closed Sat & Sun.* A.Ax.B.Dc. **££.**

Maggie Jones 1 D 8

6 Old Court Place, Kensington Church St W8. 01-937 6462. Tiny, but neat and pleasant with its scrubbed tables and country atmosphere. Home-made pâtés and

soups and good portions of plain English cooking supplemented by steak and mango casserole, and some excellent pepper steaks. Robust fresh vegetables, expertly cooked and in pleasing variety; leeks, parsnips, turnips. *LD (Reserve) open to 23.30. Closed L Sun.* A.Ax.B.Dc. **£.**

Massey's Chop House   2 I 12

38 Beauchamp Place SW3. 01-589 4856. A simple little place in a street full of restaurants and modish shops, with a cramped room at street level and a bar lounge in the basement. Straightforward steaks, chops and charcoal grills. Cheese and simple sweets to follow. Pleasant and obliging service. *LD open to 22.45. Closed Sun in the winter.* A.Ax.B.Cb.Dc. **££.**

Printer's Pie   6 L 27

60 Fleet St EC4. 01-353 8861. Simple English dishes, grills, pies, steak and kidney pudding; traditional sweets, competently prepared and not expensive, in a pleasant, vaguely Victorian, setting. *LD open to 23.00. Closed Sun, D Sat.* A.Ax.B.Dc. **£.**

Provans   4 L 4

306b Fulham Rd SW10. 01-352 7343. The elaborate pink and grey decor of this long room aptly sets off some unusual and highly imaginitive dishes on a menu changed according to season and availability. Sorrel soup, fish mousses and soufflés, turbot and scallop vol-au-vent, fillet steak in red wine with hazelnut sauce. Mr Provan's cooking is reliable and his restaurant has stood the test of time and commands a loyal following. *D (Reserve) open to 24.00.* **££.**

Rules   6 J 23

35 Maiden Lane, Strand WC2. 01-836 5314. Something of a landmark. A splendidly preserved eating house rich in literary associations. Appropriately heavy decor with an immense collection of pictures, prints, cartoons and playbills. Traditional English dishes like jugged hare, steak and kidney pie, boiled beef with carrots and dumplings, braised oxtail, seem preferable to the French and Italian offerings of the menu. On the tourist circuit, so booking essential. *LD (Reserve) open to 23.15. Closed Sat & Sun.* A.Ax.B. **££.**

Simpson's in the Strand   **6 K** 23
100 Strand WC2. 01-836 9112. This English institution
is still remarkable for the excellence of its meat. Choose
smoked salmon, eel or trout, and roast beef, duck or
saddle of mutton from the trolley, remembering to tip
the carver. The beef and mutton are unfailingly
splendid. Savouries can be had as well as proper
English puddings like treacle roll. The Stilton is reliable
and there is always vintage port by the glass to
accompany it. Fine wine list. Booking and correct dress
essential. *LD (Reserve) open to 22.00. Closed Sun.* A.B.
££.

Stone's Chop House   **5 J** 21
Panton St SW1. 01-930 0037. A modern representation
of a Victorian chop house, just off Leicester Square and
useful to the theatregoer. Soups, turbot, sole and
salmon, and a wide choice of roasts and grills,
supplemented by dishes of the day. Rib of beef with
Yorkshire pudding, saddle of mutton from the trolley,
steak and kidney pudding. Stone's sponge pancake or a
savoury to follow. *LD open to 23.15. Closed Sun.*
A.Ax.B. **££.**

Tate Gallery Restaurant   **5 P** 18
Millbank SW1. 01-834 6754. Ideally located for art

lovers on the lower ground floor of the Tate. In the Rex Whistler room, a lively lunchtime restaurant offering historical English fare and a distinguished, reasonably priced wine list. Plat du jour, veal kidneys Florentine (a dish dating back to Elizabethan times) and Joan Cromwell's grand salad are favourites. *L (Reserve) open to 15.00. Closed Sun.* **££.**

Tetther's   1 A 5

6 Portland Rd W11. 01-727 6167. Small and highly individual restaurant, many of its dishes based on the owner's research into old sources. Unusual combinations and flavours; results sometimes variable. Menu changes frequently. Pleasant atmosphere. Now a branch at 5 White Hart Lane SW13. *LD (Reserve) open to 23.00. Closed D Sun, L Sat.* A.Ax.B.Dc. **££.**

Throgmorton Restaurant   6 N 31

27 Throgmorton St EC2. 01-588 5165. A very friendly, club-like atmosphere pervades this City establishment, conveniently near the Stock Exchange and the Bank. Generous portions of roast beef, fried fish, pork, lamb, and steak and kidney pie served in the oak panelled dining room. Slightly pricier steaks and chops in the long, thin, mirrored grill room. *L (Reserve) open to 15.00. Closed Sat & Sun.* A.Ax.B.Cb.Dc. **£.**

Turpins

118 Heath St, Hampstead NW3. 01-435 3791. Pleasantly decorated restaurant in a handsome 18th century house. Unusual soups, deep fried mushrooms, best end of lamb with mango in pastry, roast beef and Yorkshire pudding, duck and cherry pie, treacle tart. Service in the garden in summer. *D (Reserve) open to 23.00. L on Sun only and during the week in summer. Closed D Sun & Mon.* A.Ax.B.Dc. **££.**

The Vine Grill   2 I 20

3 Piccadilly Place (off Swallow St) W1. 01-734 5789. Small cosy old-fashioned place in a courtyard just off Piccadilly. Owned by Bentley's round the corner in Swallow St. Lobster soup, plain steaks, chops and cutlets; the meat is of excellent quality. *LD open to 21.45. Closed Sat & Sun.* A.Ax.B.Dc. **££.**

Waltons   4 J 11

121 Walton St SW3. 01-584 0204. Very studied, rather

sumptuous decor and an unusual and ambitious table d'hôte menu of traditional English dishes. Some reputed re-creations of 18th century delights. Results are variable, with the excellence of the raw materials sometimes obscured by fussiness. The maxim 'faites simple' seems to have been overlooked. Set menus; herb pâté, terrine of chicken and sweetbreads, fish mousses, venison with wild cherries, plain steaks, game in season. Smooth and attentive service and a notable wine list especially strong in claret. *LD (Reserve) open to 23.15. Closed D Sun. (Smaller, cheaper meals at lunch and after 22.30).* A.Ax.B.Dc. **£££+.**

Wiltons   5 J 19
27 Bury St SW1. 01-930 8391. The best oysters in London and some outstanding, quality, plain cooking. Baby lobsters, crabs, salmon, sole and turbot. Chops, grills, sausages and mash, oxtail, marvellous game, pheasant, partridge, duck, woodcock. Stilton to follow. Fine wine list, good port. Charming, evocative art nouveau decor, old-fashioned standards of service. *LD (Reserve) open to 22.15. Closed Sat & Sun, D Fri.* Ax.Dc. **£££.**

Fish restaurants

Bentley's Restaurant and Oyster Bar   2 I 20
11–15 Swallow St W1. 01-734 4756. Choose here between the upstairs dining-room and the ground floor oyster bar with its long marble counter and tables in little stalls. The latter has more charm. Oysters from Bentley's own beds are excellent, with lobster, crab and good fresh fish to follow. *LD (Reserve) open to 22.45. Closed Sun.* A.Ax.B.Cb.Dc. **£££.**

Bill Bentley's   6 N 33
Swedeland Court, 202 Bishopsgate EC2. 01-283 1763. The oyster bar at street level and the luxuriously converted cellar restaurant are predictably popular with City men. Fish predominates although there is a choice of roasts and grills all carefully prepared, some lavishly sauced. Notable wine list. *L (Reserve) open to 15.00. Closed Sat & Sun.* A.Ax.B.Dc. **££.**

Le Caspia
Knightsbridge Green, 22 Brompton Rd SW1. 01-589 8772. Formerly the Caviar Bar. Owned by Viscount Newport and managed by the congenial Mr Coello, this plush yet relaxing restaurant offers some delectable fish specialities. Four types of caviar, smoked sturgeon mousse, fish pâté Trakir (sea bass and turbot with purée spinach and truffles in gelatine and tartare sauce), live lobster every day, many varieties of sole and turbot, fish soufflés. Also châteaubriand, steak tartare and Diane, veal cutlets with truffles. *LD (Reserve) open to 23.30. Closed Sun.* A.Ax.B.Cb.Dc. **£££+.**

La Croisette
168 Ifield Rd SW10. 01-373 3694. It seems an improbable thing that a specialised and expensive restaurant in a dingy street off the farther end of the Fulham Road should succeed. But Monsieur Martin's courage and enterprise have been justly rewarded. His basement restaurant is packed with fashionable people, and his second establishment opened at the end of 1976. The explanation is the excellence of the fish. There is a single fixed price menu with limited choice, but that may include the now celebrated plateau de fruits de mer, marvellous soupe de poissons, langoustines, daurade, rougets en papillote, loup grillé au fenouil, with cheeses, fruit tarts and oeufs à la neige to follow. The Mètaireau Muscadet is fresh and attractive, and the service French and effective. *LD open to 23.15. Closed Mon, L Tues. Set meal.* **£££.**

Cunninghams Oyster Bar
17b Curzon St W1. 01-499 7595. Established in Curzon Street since 1723 and still run by the Cunningham family. Elegant period decor, real paintings and always fresh flowers on the tables. Sole prepared in 20 different ways. Good oysters, turbot, halibut, salmon. Lobsters are the highlight of the menu and offered in 12 varieties. *LD (Reserve) open to 23.00.* A.Ax.B.Cb.Dc. **£££.**

Geale's Fish Restaurant
2–4 Farmer St W8. 01-727 7969. A simple, informal little restaurant with cheerful service and tearoom atmosphere. Good fish, all popular varieties, and real chips; crab soup, the odd pudding, and eight wines by

the glass. Additional seating upstairs with a bar. *LD open to 22.45. Closed Sun, Mon.* **£.**

Golden Carp 2 G 17
8a Mount St W1. 01-499 3385. Downstairs modern, elegant Mayfair restaurant in the same ownership as the Marquis across the street. There are carp dishes among the more commonly found sole, turbot, crab and lobster. Also an oyster bar. For the timorous there is also a wide choice of meat and poultry. *LD open to 23.30. Closed Sun, L Sat.* A.Ax.B.Dc. **££.**

Gow's 6 N 32
81 Old Broad St EC2. 01-628 0530. Old fashioned oyster bar and simple restaurant justly popular with City folk. Good fish and good value. Controlled by Balls Bros, as is indicated by the extensive wine list. *L open to 15.00. Closed Sat & Sun.* A.B. **£.**

Manzi's 2 I 22
1–2 Leicester St WC2. 01-437 4864. An old established restaurant on two floors. Manzi's offers a wide range of fish and shellfish but simpler dishes such as salmon or turbot grilled or poached seem the wisest choice. In keeping with the place's Italian origins there is authentic zabaglione to follow. Service is bustling and erratic. *LD (Reserve) open to 23.45. Closed L Sun.* A.Ax.B.Cb.Dc. **££.**

Overton's 5 J 19
5 St James's St SW1. 01-839 3774. The dignified bow-windowed façade shelters a sedate, traditional restaurant with the unhurried atmosphere of a vanished age. There is a handsome oyster bar for relatively quick meals and beyond it, a cocktail bar and the restaurant proper. Straightforward menu of familiar fish dishes prepared from first-class raw materials. Notable oysters and lobsters. Crêpes, a sweet omelette or perhaps a savoury to follow. Service is of exemplary politeness. Fine wine list. *LD (Reserve) open to 23.00. Closed Sun.* A.Ax.B.Dc. **££.**

Poissonnerie de l'Avenue 4 K 11
82 Sloane Avenue SW3. 01-589 2457. Cheerful French restaurant with an intimate atmosphere. Less cramped nowadays with the opening of the upstairs room. Dependable cooking. A variety of good fresh fish: sole,

turbot, brill, halibut, mackerel, smoked haddock. Oysters, mussels and scallops in season and a bouillabaisse maison. Pleasant white wines, good cheeses and well made sweets. *LD (Reserve) open to 23.30. Closed Sun.* A.Ax.B.Dc. **££**.

Scott's 2 G 17
20 Mount St W1. 01-629 5248. Formerly a luxurious Edwardian restaurant in Piccadilly Circus, now in comfortable modern premises. Although the decor is not to everyone's taste, tradition is maintained by splendid oysters and fresh, skilfully cooked fish. Plats du jour lend variety to the menu with a useful list of entrées and grills, sweetbreads, tournedos, cutlets and plain steaks. But fish remains the speciality; the salmon, turbot, crab and lobster are memorable. Impeccable service and good wine list. *LD (Reserve) open to 22.45. Closed L Sun.* A.Ax.B.Dc. **£££**.

Sheekey's 5 J 22
28 St Martin's Court WC2. 01-836 4118. For the three hundred odd years of its existence this well-loved restaurant was run by the family of its founder. Now, part of the Scott's group who have endeavoured to maintain its long tradition, specialities continue to be oysters, lobsters and turbot cooked in a variety of ways. Situated in the heart of theatreland. Hopefully the good value and happy, informal atmosphere which for so long have characterised this simple restaurant will

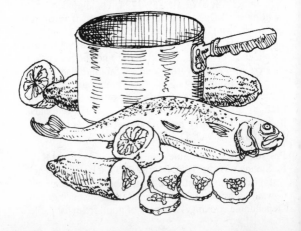

survive to delight the theatre-goer. *LD open to. 23.30. Closed Sun.* A.Ax.B.Dc. **££**.

Le Suquet
4 K 11

104 Draycott Avenue SW3. 01-581 1785. The second of M. Martin's fish restaurants. Warm and bustling; relaxed atmosphere. A la carte menu, the main feature being the massive plateau de fruits de mer. Loup grillé au fenouil is another speciality well worth trying. Efficient, helpful service with true Gallic charm. Good wine list. *LD (Reserve) open to 23.15. Closed Mon, L Tues.* Ax. **£££**.

Sweeting's
6 N 29

39 Queen Victoria St EC2. 01-248 3062. Scrubbed tables and seats at the bar. Rudimentary comfort, but splendid oysters, salmon, fish pie, fishcakes, herrings with mustard, and turbot, all simply prepared. Good cheeses, savouries and traditional puddings served by staff with appropriately old-fashioned courtesy. Muscadet en carafe, Black velvet, good port. Very popular, and queueing often necessary. *L open to 14.30. Closed Sat & Sun.* **£**.

Wheeler's Fish Restaurants

The origins of this well-known chain go back over a hundred and twenty years to the fish shop in Old Compton Street which today is one of 11 Wheeler's restaurants in London. These are well placed in the City, Soho, Mayfair, Belgravia and Kensington and though each has its own character, there are certain points of similarity: green painted exteriors, leaded windows, panelling, red plush, pictures, prints and ornaments, often oyster bars, and always excellent fish and shellfish. The family identity is further maintained by menus broadly uniform, with oysters, mussels, scallops, smoked salmon, smoked eel or potted shrimps to start, turbot, plaice, salmon or lobster prepared in a variety of ways to follow, with fruit or a piece of cheese to finish.

The fish is fresh and well prepared. If sauces are rarely miraculous, equally seldom is the fish spoiled by over cooking. Service is bustling, cheerful, prompt and generally friendly, and the restaurants inspire fierce loyalty. *LD (Reserve) open to 23.00. Closing days vary.* A.Ax.B.Cb.Dc. **££**.

Alcove   1 D 4
17 Kensington High St W8. 01-937 1443.

Antoine's   2 F 22
40 Charlotte St W1. 01-636 2817.

Braganza   2 H 22
56 Frith St W1. 01-437 5412.

Carafe   5 J 13
15 Lowndes St SW1. 01-235 2525.

George & Dragon   1 I 11
256 Brompton Rd SW3. 01-584 2626.

Sovereign   2 I 16
17 Hertford St W1. 01-499 4679.

Vendôme   2 I 19
20 Dover St W1. 01-629 5417.

Wheeler's   2 I 22
19 Old Compton St W1. 01-437 2706.

Wheeler's   5 J 20
12a Duke of York St SW1. 01-930 2460.

Wheeler's City Restaurant   6 P 31
19–21 Great Tower St EC3. 01-626 3685.

Wheeler's   6 O 31
9–13 Fenchurch Buildings EC3. 01-488 4848.

French

The following restaurants all serve classical French dishes. Some specialise in simple French provincial food, others in very sophisticated cuisine. You will find here some of the best cooking in the world.

L'Artiste Affamé   1 I 5
243 Old Brompton Rd SW5. 01-373 1659. A long list of straightforward provincial dishes, adequately prepared and enjoyable. Oeufs Bénédictine, saucissons assortis, crespaline maison—crêpe filled with spinach, nuts and sultanas in a Parmesan sauce, filet Dijon, veal with rosemary. Plain surroundings enhanced by 'rustic' antiques and a welcoming log fire downstairs in winter. *LD open to 23.15. Closed Sun, L Sat.* A.Ax.B.Dc. **££**.

L'Artiste Assoiffé   1 A 8
122 Kensington Park Rd W11. 01-727 5111. Informal

and very worthwhile. A typical Kensington corner house close to the antique shops of the Portobello Road. Candlelight and the rather long intervals between courses, create a leisurely atmosphere. Fairly authentic French food well cooked. Fondue bourguignonne, entrecôte au poivre, chicken stuffed with mushrooms in pastry, foie de veau des gourmets. *D open to 23.30. Sat L only. Closed Sun.* A.Ax.B.Cb.Dc. **££**.

L'Aubergade

816 Finchley Rd, Temple Fortune NW11. 01-455 8853. This authentic French restaurant is just north of Golders Green among the semi-detached mansions of the new executives. Bistro decor and atmosphere; a short menu supplemented by dishes of the day. Soupe de Provence, escalope de veau au citron, sorbets, crêpes. Careful cooking and attentive service have given this simple place a strong local following. *D open to 23.00. Closed Sun.* Ax.B.Dc. **££**.

Bagatelle   4 L 5

5 Langton St SW10. 01-351 4185. Soothing, relaxed atmosphere to be found in this charming out of the way restaurant. On both floors the decor is simple pale creamy white walls. Service is friendly and efficient. Fish soup, croustade de fruits de mer, duck pâté, filet of sole, tarte aux pommes, sorbet or a good selection of cheeses. *LD (Reserve D) open to 23.30. Closed Sun.* A.Ax.B.Dc. **££**.

Berkeley Hotel Restaurant   2 I 14

Wilton Place SW1. 01-235 6000. This strikingly decorated room in mauve and white provides an appropriately stylish setting for French cuisine of consistent excellence. Many of the dishes represent the able chef's variations on classical themes. Raw materials of the first quality are prepared with great finesse. Notable wine list and service of exemplary courtesy. *LD (Reserve) open to 23.30. Closed Sun.* A. **£££**.

Bewick's   4 J 11

87 Walton St SW3. 01-584 6711. Decorated in green suede and the walls lined with framed Hermès scarves. The food remains mainly French and well prepared.

Carré d'agneau au poivre vert a speciality, poulet au citron, tournedos béarnaise. Good fresh vegetables and a rich mousse au chocolat. *LD open to 23.00. Closed L Sun.* A.Ax.B.Cb. **££.**

Au Bois St Jean

122 St John's Wood High St NW8. 01-722 0400. Intimate bistro atmosphere on two floors with a set menu at lunch only. The kitchen staff are French and there is plenty of flavour to the cooking. Freshly made plats du jour, terrine de montagne. Informal and enjoyable. *LD (Reserve) open to 23.30. Closed Sun.* A.Ax.B.Dc. **££.**

Au Bon Accueil   4 K 10

27 Elystan St SW3. 01-589 3718. For long a favourite of Chelsea residents. Two cramped and plainly decorated rooms at street level, a third, tiny, downstairs by the kitchen. Good unpretentious cooking. A choice of oeufs en cocotte, seafood in crêpes, coquilles, mussels, veal with rum and orange, jugged hare, filet mignon with excellent béarnaise. Fairly priced wine list, palatable carafes. Bustling and cheerful. Six tables outside in summer. *LD (Reserve D) open to 23.30 Closed Sun, L Sat.* A.Ax.Dc. **££.**

Boulestin   6 J 23

25 Southampton St WC2. 01-836 7061. Although the great days of the Boulestin are long gone, under new management and with complete refurbishment, this memorable restaurant is experiencing a new lease of life. The three magnificent chandeliers remain but while the menu retains some of the original dishes, there are many new and interesting specialities. Pavé la villette au poivre rose, escalope de ris de veau aux felaments des safrans, crabe aux artichauts Boulestin. Fine wines; dignified service. *LD open to 23.15. Closed Sun, L Sat.* A.Ax.B.Cb.Dc. **£££+.**

La Brasserie   4 J 10

272 Brompton Rd SW3. 01-584 1668. The former 'Elegant Bistro' has a great deal more elegance nowadays. Drink at the long bar or eat at a table under a potted palm. Conventional menu, dishes of the day, omelettes, blanquette de veau, avocados stuffed with

smoked salmon and celery, all competently enough prepared though lacking real distinction. Open throughout the day for coffee and pâtisserie— newspapers provided. *LD open to 23.00*. Ax.B.Dc. **££**.

Brasserie des Amis 2 I 13

27 Basil St SW3. 01-584 9012. Bustling newcomer to the brasserie scene. Brightly decorated with mirrors, green wicker-work furniture and plenty of plants. If alone, you can eat at the bar. Good, reliable French provençale cooking in the same tradition as the sister restaurant (Mes Amis) although considerably cheaper. *LD open to 22.30*. A.Ax.B.Dc. **£**.

Brasserie du Coin 3 H 26

54 Lamb's Conduit St WC1. 01-405 1717. Refreshingly bare and not very expensive. Quick meals at the counter. Adequate choice of French dishes well prepared and tempting plats du jour, civet de lièvre, steak au poivre and good cheeses. Predictably busy at lunchtime. *LD (Reserve L) open to 22.30. Closed Sat & Sun*. A.Ax.Dc. **££**.

Le Bressan 1 E 7

14 Wrights Lane W8. 01-937 8525. Elegantly decorated rooms in a converted house off Kensington High St provide the setting for some very good cooking. Classical French menu varied by the chef's suggestions. Hare pâté, oeufs en meurette, and a splendid array of French cheeses. *LD (Reserve) open to 23.30. Closed Sat & Sun and Aug–Sep*. A.Ax.B.Dc. **£££**.

Bubb's 6 K 29

329 Central Market EC1. 01-236 2435. A pleasing escape from the bustle of Smithfields Market. Popular with City gents. On two floors; downstairs is quieter. Plain and simple decor, with a few posters on the walls. Great care is taken in preparing the food, so service can be very slow. Fish pâté, onion soup, escargots, sweetbreads fried in pastry, calf's liver provençale. Excellent desserts and cheeseboard. *LD (Reserve) open to 21.30. Closed Sat, Sun*. A.B.Dc. **££**.

Le Café Royal

72 High St Wimbledon SW19. 01-946 0238. There is a pleasant, cottagey atmosphere about this simple little restaurant on two floors. Quite an extensive menu, with

most emphasis on chicken and veal, the dishes soundly enough prepared. Good fresh vegetables. Attentive service. *LD open to 22.30. Closed Sun.* A.Ax.B.Dc. **££.**

Café Royal Grill Room 2 I 20
68 Regent St W1. 01-437 9090. The extravagant rococo decor of the grill remains with its mirrors, caryatids, gilding and painted ceiling just as it was in the days of Whistler, Wilde and Beardsley. The menu is long and ambitious, many of the dishes resoundingly named—quenelles de turbot Bonne Bouche, noisette de veau Argenteuil, côtelettes d'agneau farcis Brixham, scampi Oscar Wilde. There is simpler fare—carré d'agneau persillé, ris de veau Clamart, and game in season. Service is formal and the cellar remarkable. *LD (Reserve) open to 23.30. Closed alternate L Sat.* A.Ax.B.Cb.Dc. **£££.**

Café Royal, Le Relais 2 I 20
68 Regent St W1. 01-930 6611. Large and luxurious, with interesting and typically French fare featuring a three course fixed price menu. Salad Melinda, oeufs en cocotte Chambertin, blanquette de lotte Honfleur, foie de caneton sur tartine, soufflé Grand Marnier. Also Sunday brunch. *LD open to 23.00. Closed alternate L Sat.* A.Ax.B.Cb.Dc. **£££.**

Capability Brown
351 West End Lane NW6. 01-794 3234. Interesting restaurant in West Hampstead. On the ground floor there is a small bar and a spiral staircase leads down into the dining area. Brightly decorated with floral tablecloths and lightly coloured walls. Cuisine Minceur is served here. For starters melon and grapefruit cocktail with fresh mint or terrine de légumes chaudes. To follow chicken stuffed with a mixture of minced chicken, spices, onions and mushrooms steamed in their own juices served with a purée of watercress sauce. Finally, pear with banana and strawberry purée topped with almonds served hot. *LD (Reserve) open to 23.30. Closed Sun, L Sat.* A.B. **££.**

Capital Hotel Restaurant 2 I 13
22 Basil St SW3. 01-589 5171. This modern hotel's modest façade shelters one of London's outstanding restaurants. Improbably the chef is English, but the

delicacy and finesse of his cooking is undoubtedly
French. Featherlight quenelles, mousseline de coquilles
St Jacques, médaillon de veau à la Biscayenne, carré
d'agneau persillé, gratin dauphinoise, marvellous
sorbets. *LD (Reserve) open to 22.30.* A.Ax.B.Cb.Dc.
£££.

Carlo's Place   4 K 1
855 Fulham Rd SW6. 01-736 4507. Cheerful bistro
miles down the Fulham Rd, decorated with cuckoo
clocks, stove pipes and naked bulbs. Sound French and
English cooking: goujons de sole, crêpes de crevettes,
carré d'agneau, marinated mackerel with chilli or plain
roast duck; all well prepared and attractively presented.
Short wine list, with usually one or two good bottles on
special offer. Mannered, attentive service. *LD (Reserve)
open to 23.15. Closed Mon.* **££**.

Cellier du Midi
28 Church Row NW3. 01-435 9998. A white-walled
cellar of a Hampstead cottage with typical bistro decor
and cooking; highly seasoned, strongly flavoured and
sometimes unevenly prepared. Snails, pot au feu,
noisette de veau, crème brûlée. *D (Reserve) open to
23.30. Closed Sun.* A.Ax.B.Cb.Dc. **££**.

Chelsea Room, Carlton Tower   5 K 13
Cadogan Place SW1. 01-235 5411. A handsome
modern room overlooking the gardens of Cadogan
Place, with cocktail bar and pianist at the farther end.
This is the formal restaurant of the hotel. The ambitious
menu is largely French with coquilles St Jacques au
safran, escalope de saumon à l'oseille, entrecôte à la
moëlle, coq au Brouilly among many tempting dishes.
Service is friendly and well-meaning and the wine list
distinguished. Worth noting here are the gastronomic
festivals held from time to time with visiting chefs. *LD
(Reserve) open to 23.00.* A.Ax.B.Cb.Dc. **£££+**.

Chez Gerard   2 F 22
5 Charlotte St W1. 01-636 4975. Simple and appealing.
Now open upstairs as well, the menu is sensibly short,
with most emphasis on charcoal grills. Adequate hors
d'oeuvre, escalope de veau, châteaubriand, and a good
choice of sweets from the trolley. *LD (Reserve) open to
23.00. Closed L Sat.* A.B. **£**.

Claridge's Restaurant   2 G 18

Brook St W1. 01-629 8860. A charming, comfortable 1930s style room decorated in pastel colours. The menu is formal and wide-ranging, the dishes often prepared with skill and always from the best of raw materials. The wine list begins with 29 varieties of champagne. In the evening, the gipsy music from outside may strike you as comic or romantic according to your mood. Friendly, courteous service. *LD (Reserve) open to 23.00.* A. **£££.**

La Crémaillère

148 Lordship Lane SE22. 01-693 8266. Discreet new restaurant in a residential area, previously the site of Chez Nico. Two young French partners offering authentic French cuisine. Limited menu changes regularly. Mousse de poisson with sauce aurore, oeufs aux cocottes au paprika, blanquette de veau à l'ancien, le poulet Normande, filet de boeuf sauce Henri IV. Delicious desserts all home-made. French cheeses, fine wine list. *D open to 22.30. Closed Sun, Mon.* **£££.**

Daphne's   4 K 11

112 Draycott Avenue SW3. 01-589 4257. Small and intimate with subdued lighting and a very relaxed

atmosphere. A strong local following who appreciate the consistently good cooking of the wide-ranging menu and the blackboard plats du jour. Poulet fumé et avocat, good fish and game, carré d'agneau, médaillon de boeuf au poivre vert, fresh vegetables. To finish, try the soufflé Grand Marnier. A fine wine list. *D (Reserve) open to 24.00. Closed Sun.* A.Ax.B.Dc. **££.**

Eatons   5 L 14
49 Elizabeth St SW1. 01-730 0074. An intimate atmosphere exudes from this attractive, small French restaurant. The service is courteous and helpful. For starters watercress and potato soup, smoked trout or blinis. To follow either chicken suprême, lamb and kidneys provençale, pork escalope—stuffed with red cabbage and raisins; finally a selection of home-made cakes or fresh fruit salad from the trolley. *LD (Reserve) open to 23.00. Closed Sat, Sun.* A.Ax.Dc. **££.**

A L'Ecu de France   2 I 19
111 Jermyn St SW1. 01-930 2837. Though the Empress and the Old Caprice are no more, this traditional restaurant, formal and luxurious, remains unchanging. The menu is wide-ranging and ambitious and results generally satisfactory; fruits de mer, ris de veau paysanne and a fine cold table. Notable wine list. Much used for business entertaining. *LD open to 23.30. Closed L Sat. L Sun.* A.Ax.B.Dc. **£££.**

L'Escargot Bienvenu   2 H 22
48 Greek St W1. 01-437 4460. Engagingly old fashioned decor and a sedate atmosphere distinguish this long established restaurant bourgeois. Snails, fresh sardines, coquilles St Jacques meunière, saucisses de Toulouse, haricots blancs, carbonnade de boeuf flamande. Well chosen wine list, especially strong in Alsace. *LD (Reserve) open to 22.30. Closed Sun, L Sat.* A.Ax.B.Cb.Dc. **££.**

L'Etoile   2 F 22
30 Charlotte St W1. 01-636 7189. A Soho institution; a notable restaurant with appropriately formal service of reliable dishes. Turbot monégasque, tête de veau vinaigrette, crab, lobster, rognons sautés au vin rouge, ris de veau aux champignons, cervelles panées, roast duck, quail or guineafowl. Invariably packed at

lunchtime. Splendid wine list. *LD (Reserve) open to 22.00. Closed Sat & Sun.* Ax.Dc. **£££.**

Au Fin Bec 4 K 11

100 Draycott Avenue SW3. 01-584 3600. It is difficult to get into this restaurant, an indication of the quality of the cooking as well of its size. Interesting and authentic dishes; mousse de foie Strasbourg, oeufs Bénédictine, supreme de volaille à l'estragon, steak Diane, good fresh vegetables and well-made zabaglione. *LD (Reserve) open to 23.00. Closed Sun.* A.Ax.B.Dc. **££.**

Le Français 4 K 7

259 Fulham Rd SW3. 01-352 3668. A serious restaurant with two menus: a fixed carte of well chosen French dishes, reliably executed, and a selection—changed every week—of specialities of individual provinces, accompanied by appropriate wines. Some provinces have a cuisine of greater appeal than others, but here you can make a gastronomic tour de France without going farther afield than the Fulham Road. Fine wine list and polished service. *LD open to 23.00. Closed Sun.* Ax.Dc. **£££.**

Le Gavroche 5 M 12

61–63 Lower Sloane St SW1. 01-730 2820. One of the best restaurants in London, presided over by the Roux brothers and renowned for its luxurious atmosphere and almost faultless 'haute cuisine'. Soufflé suissesse, oeufs carème, sole soufflé, rognons de veau aux trois moutardes, caneton Gavroche or Juliette, excellent pâtisserie. Service polished and courteous. Magnificent wine list regrettably rather highly priced. *D (Reserve) open to 24.00. Closed Sun.* Dc.Ax. **£££+**

Geneviève 2 E 19

13 Thayer St W1. 01-486 2244. Satisfactory cuisine bourgeoise in comfortable surroundings. Coq au vin, médaillon de veau aux morilles. Long, well chosen wine list. *LD open to 23.00. Closed Sun, L Sat.* A.Ax.B.Dc. **££.**

La Germainerie 6 J 26

120 Chancery Lane WC2. 01-405 0290. Simple dishes in a cellar with wooden tables and a pleasant atmosphere. Agreeable and not expensive. *LD open to 22.30. Closed Sat & Sun.* A.B. **££.**

Ici Paris   2 E 18

2a Duke St W1. 01-935 1864. Decor in blue and gold
lends a touch of luxury to this cosy little restaurant.
Familiar dishes competently prepared; pâtés, onion
soup, carré d'agneau à la Corse, tarte maison. Pianist
nightly. *LD open to 22.30. Closed Sun, L Sat.*
A.Ax.B.Dc. **££.**

Au Jardin des Gourmets   2 H 22

5 Greek St W1. 01-437 1816. Famous for many years
for its cellar which still shelters claret old and rare.
Ambitious menu and sometimes variable results. Snails,
clams baked in champagne and cream sauce, canard
rôti aux olives; very good cheese board to follow. *LD
(Reserve) open to 23.30. Closed Sun, L Sat.*
A.Ax.B.Dc. **££.**

Keats

Downshire Hill, Hampstead NW3. 01-435 1499.
Colourful decor matched by an elaborate and complex
fortnightly menu. The cooking can be very good, and
some of the seasonal specialities are admirably done.
Twelve-dish bookable feasts for gourmets at Christmas
and other times during the year. Notable wine list. *D
(Reserve) open to 24.00. Sun L.* A.Ax.B.Dc. **£££.**

Langan's Brasserie   2 I 18

Stratton St W1. 01-493 6437. Opened by Peter Langan
and Michael Caine on the site of the former Coq d'Or.
Vast L-shaped room with a rather glittering, carefully
contrived atmosphere of decaying splendour. Always
busy, a very fashionable place to see and be seen in.
Changing menu. Erratic service. Live music every
night. *LD (Reserve) open to 23.00. Closed Sun, L Sat.*
Ax.Dc. **££.**

Ma Cuisine   4 J 11

113 Walton St SW3. 01-584 7585. This little restaurant
is the personal creation of Guy Mouilleron, a native of
South Western France, who set up on his own after a
dozen years in leading London restaurants. The room is
small, comfortable and simply decorated. The menu is
short, full of interest with such dishes as mousseline de
coquilles Saint Jacques à l'orange, langoustines à
l'oseille, ballotine de volaille Lucien Teudret—the
crabmeat stuffing especially delicious; noisettes

d'agneau pastourelle, lamb of marvellous quality served with a purée of onion and mint. Everything is beautifully presented, appealing to the eye as well as the palate. The service is courteous and effective, but the wine list lacks distinction. Undoubtedly Ma Cuisine is currently among the very best of London's restaurants; it is advisable to book a table for dinner several weeks in advance. *LD (Reserve) open 23.00. Closed Sat & Sun.* Ax.Dc. **£££+**.

Marcel 2 I 13
14 Sloane St SW1. 01-235 4912. Two cheerful rooms characterised by their rustic decor and gleaming copper. Extensive cold table and glimpses of kitchen activity at the back of the room prompt expectations which are sustained by very satisfactory results. The menu offers a wide choice of familiar French dishes, supplemented by special dishes of the day. Seasonal specialities are chalked on the blackboard. Service is friendly and bustling. The restaurant is justly popular with Knightsbridge shoppers and booking is advisable. *LD (Reserve) open to 23.00. Closed Sun.* Ax.Dc. **£££**.

Le Marmiton 6 M 32
4 Blomfield St EC2. 01-588 4643. Very close to Liverpool St, a crowded informal City restaurant with booths upstairs for confidential discussions. Adequate cooking and prompt, obliging service. Quiches, terrines, sole meunière, rognons Bercy, French cheeses. *L (Reserve) open to 14.45. Closed Sat & Sun.* **££**.

Mes Amis 2 I 13
31 Basil St SW3 (corner of Hans Rd). 01-584 9099. Tasteful proprietor-run restaurant. Heavy wooden beams and rough whitewashed walls on the ground floor restaurant with leafy hanging baskets. Vaulted though cramped and rather warm basement room with a view into the garden. High standard of provençal farmhouse cooking—aubergines with ham slices baked with cheese and herbs, carré d'agneau au poivre vert and cassollette are among the specialities. The very large portions match the very high prices. Charming bar for aperitifs. Excellent, thoughtful service. Comprehensive wine list. *LD open to 23.00.* A.Ax.B.Dc. **£££**.

M'sieur Frog 3 E 33

31a Essex Rd N1. 01-226 3495. Charming, small restaurant in converted building. Small bar near the entrance, walls are a rich mahogany colour with pine beams. Very popular with the local residents of Islington. For starters choose either potage crecy—carrot, onion and chervil soup; cold stuffed tomatoes with crab, avocado and celery and, of course, frogs legs cooked with fresh herbs and white wine. To follow rabbit casserole with mushrooms, onions and bacon; lamb cutlets with cheese stuffing or duckling with green peppercorns. They have an excellent cheeseboard. Reasonable selection of wines. *D (Reserve) open to 23.00. Closed Sun.* **££.**

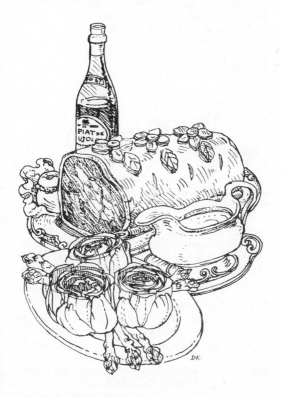

Mon Plaisir   3 I 23
21 Monmouth St WC2. 01-836 7243. Small, spartan,
typically French bistro. Unobsequious but friendly
service. Conveniently close to the theatres. Escalope à
l'estragon, veau marengo, poulet au vinaigre. Wine in
carafes. *LD (Reserve) open to 23.00. Closed Sat & Sun.*
£.

Le Mont St Michel
282 Uxbridge Rd W12. 01-749 5412. Authentic
French cooking in this family-run restaurant. Stark
white walls, red chairs and fresh red and white linen
tablecloths. Soft background music. Try the delicious
home-made pâtés, rabbit roasted in white wine or veal
provençale. To follow crème brûlée, gâteau du jour or a
fine selection of cheeses. Slow service. *LD open to
23.30. Closed Sun, L Sat.* A.Ax.B.Dc. **££.**

Montcalm, La Varenne   2 D 16
Great Cumberland Place W1. 01-402 4288. An elegant
restaurant in this unobtrusive Georgian-style hotel.
Choose between the excellent value of the fixed-price
menu or the carte proper. Billi-bi, marvellous quenelles,
poussin en papillote, a tempting sweet trolley. *LD
(Reserve) open to 22.30.* A.Ax.B.Cb.Dc. **£££.**

L'Opéra   3 I 24
32 Gt Queen St WC2. 01-405 9020. A plush,
elaborately decorated though intimate restaurant
appropriately close to Covent Garden. French dishes
predominate on the wide-ranging menu and though the
cooking, like the service, can be variable, results are
generally satisfactory. Bouillabaisse, moules marinière,
haddock mousse, entrecôte bordelaise, chevreuil aux
cerises, and a predictably excellent wine list. *LD
(Reserve) open to 24.00. Closed L Sat, Sun.*
A.Ax.B.Dc. **££.**

Le Petit Montmartre   2 D 19
15 Marylebone Lane W1. 01-935 9226. Cheerful
decor, a warm welcome and sound cooking of good raw
materials make this an appealing restaurant. Oeufs en
cocotte, cassoulet Toulousain, rognons de veau au
Madère, entrecôte Café de Paris—covered in butter, a
mixture of 24 herbs and brandy, good fresh vegetables.
A useful spot in which to fortify oneself against the

rigours of Harley St. *LD (Reserve) open to 23.00. Closed Sun, L Sat.* A.Ax.B.Dc. **££.**

Le Petit Prince
5 Holmes Rd NW5. 01-267 0752. Simple and appealing French-style café in Kentish Town. Small and plainly decorated, mirrors have the Little Prince painted on them and the wooden tables are bare. Serves mainly cous-cous either on its own, or with a selection of meat dishes. Otherwise try their plat du jour which might be chicken provençale or boeuf bourguignonne. To follow fresh fruit salad or home-made ice-cream. All ingredients are fresh. *D (Reserve) open to 23.30.* **£.**

Le Poulbot 6 M 29
45 Cheapside EC2. 01-236 4379. City partner of Le Gavroche. First-class raw materials, meticulous attention to detail, and great finesse in saucing make this one of the top French restaurants in London. Expense account lunches downstairs and less expensive fare upstairs. Soupe au cresson, casserolette d'escargots, poulet de Bresse. Polished, attentive service and a fine rather expensive wine list. *L (Reserve) open to 15.00. Closed Sat & Sun.* Ax.Dc. **£££.**

La Poule au Pot 5 L 14
231 Ebury St SW1. 01-730 7763. A cheerful crowded restaurant on the fringe of Belgravia. Limited menu at lunchtime, a wider and more interesting range of dishes in the evening. Ratatouille, mousse de poisson, carbonnade de boeuf, poule au pot, rabbit with mustard, the dishes are robust and satisfying. *LD (Reserve) open to 23.15. Closed Sun.* A.Ax.B. **£££.**

Au Provencal
295 Railton Rd SE24. 01-274 9163. Fine French provincial cooking in a popular local restaurant with strong Gallic overtones. Owner Trevor Keith also runs a Wine and Dine Gourmet Club on the premises. For hors d'oeuvres, salade niçoise, home-made pâté, soupe de poissons. Generous main dishes often include quenelles of pike, casserole pigeon, French farm chicken cooked with tarragon. Grand Marnier ice-cream to follow. Medium-priced wine list. *D (Reserve) open to 22.30. Closed Sun.* A. **££.**

Au Savarin 2 F 22
8 Charlotte St W1. 01-636 7134. Faded decor and a

formal atmosphere in this charming relic of a vanished age. Comprehensive French carte, strong in egg and fish dishes. Poulet poché au riz, entrecôte marchand de vin, rognons sautés au vin rouge, foie de veau au lard and a wide choice of desserts. Starched service. *LD open to 22.30 Closed Sun.* A.Ax.Dc. **££.**

Snooty Fox   **2 I 16**
52 Hertford St, Shepherd Market W1. 01-629 1786. Set menu, with supplementary charges, at lunch and dinner in this richly decorated Mayfair restaurant. Cooking is French and lavishly seasoned. Suprême de volaille à l'Estragon, bisque de crabes, duchesse de saumon, daube, entrecôte de champignons, crêpes or pâtisserie to finish. Attentive service. *LD (Reserve) open to 24.00. Closed L Sat, Sun.* Ax.B.Dc. **££.**

Le Soufflé   **2 I 16**
Inter-Continental Hotel, Hamilton Place W1. 01-409 3131. Deep red decor with subdued, candle-lit tables and decorative rose arrangements. Pleasant bar; a pianist provides the entertainment. First try the smoked salmon and avocado or langoustine soufflé. To follow, select from the international menu; boeuf au bouzy— marinated in wine and served with shallots; filet de boeuf aux trois poivres— peppered and flambé; grilled salmon with onion sauce. The accompanying vegetables are served as soufflés: spinach or potato are recommended. To end the meal, select either the hot chocolate, lemon or mixed liqueur soufflé which includes kirsh, rum, kummel and Grand Marnier. Distinguished wine list. *LD (Reserve D) open to 23.30* A.Ax.B.Dc. **£££+.**

Tante Claire   **4 N 10**
68 Royale Hospital Road SW3. 01-352 6045. Opened in 1978 by a husband and wife team, this long, narrow restaurant with its colourful walls and Klimt prints offers good, light French cuisine. The starting speciality is andouillette de la mer au vinaigre de Cassis. To follow—foie de veau au citron vert, pig's trotters stuffed with sweetbreads and morilles mushrooms. Two or three fish dishes changed daily. Delectable desserts include feuilleté aux poires which takes some time to prepare. *LD (Reserve) open to 23.00. Closed Sat & Sun.* Ax. **£££+.**

Thierry's   **4 L** 7
342 King's Rd SW3. 01-352 3365. One of the more
rewarding restaurants in the King's Road. French
proprietor and authentic cooking. Robust dishes like
cassoulet and saddle of hare. Spinach tart, moules,
soufflé au fromage. Interesting wines and sometimes
preoccupied service. *LD (Reserve D) open to 23.30.*
Closed Sun. Ax.B.Dc. **££.**

Thomas de Quincey   **6 J** 23
36 Tavistock Street, WC2. 01-240 3972. In the original
house of the 19th century opium-eating author, a stylish
restaurant with a remarkable collection of paintings,
Victorian chairs and rear garden. First floor private
room has a glass roof. Imaginative menu prepared by
an English chef, previously at the Connaught Hotel.
Try pâté de turbot, petit jambonneau de canard, or
avocado stuffed with scampi and served with curry
sauce and a poppadom to start. Main dishes include
saumon soufflé Thomas de Quincey and paume de ris
de veau Paloise. Sorbets between courses. *LD (Reserve)*
open to 23.15. Closed Sun, L Sat. A.Ax.B.Dc. **£££.**

La Toque Blanche   **1 E** 6
21 Abingdon Rd W8. 01-937 5832. A long established
restaurant, chic but cramped, that sustains its
reputation well. The chef proprietor is from Nice. Soupe
de poissons, crêpes de fruits de mer, langoustines à ma
façon, ballotine de volaille, escalope de veau
Normande. Cream sauces are liberally used. The
cheeses here are justly celebrated and the wine list
carries some fine bottles. *LD (Reserve) open to 22.45.*
Closed Sat & Sun. Ax.Dc. **££.**

White House Restaurant   **2 C** 22
Albany St NW1. 01-387 1200. Pleasing modern decor,
still-life paintings and gentle ambience enhanced by
candlelight in the evenings. Summer and winter menus.
Justifiable reputation for ably prepared fish dishes.
Dressed crab claws with American sauce, trois
poissons fumés royales, pike quenelles avec sauce au
champagne. Rich meat specialities too—carré
d'agneau salardaise, grenadine de veau flambé au
poivre vert, mignon de boeuf Sarah Bernhardt. Own
pâtisserie; good wine list. *LD (Reserve) open to 23.30.*
Closed Sun, L Sat. A.Ax.B.Cb.Dc. **££.**

German and Austrian

German food can be the most filling of all—dumplings, noodles, sausages, huge marinated roasts plus puddings and torte that are a treat for the sweetest tooth. To this, Austrians add a flair for attractive presentation, seen in creations like Sachertorte, a confection of cream, eggs, chocolate and rum. Stews are marinated or simmered for a long time to tenderise the meat—roladen or sauerbraten are the best examples. Not only wine, but beer, vinegar or lemon are used to enrich the flavour, while Wiener schnitzels are beaten out flat to ensure the tender, wafer thin breadcrumbed result.

Cosmo
5 Northways Parade, Finchley Rd NW3. 01-722 1398. German-born proprietor. Large, bright old-fashioned restaurant with a less expensive café next door, renowned for its delicious croissants and coffee at breakfast. German specialities form the bulk of the menu: frankfurters with sauerkraut, rheinischer sauerbraten, delicious schnitzel. Apfelstrudel with cream to follow. Fast attentive service. German beers or wine. *LD open to 23.00.* A.Ax.B.Dc. **£**.

Kerzenstuberl
2 E 18

9 St Christopher's Place W1. 01-486 3196. Authentic Austrian food; accordion playing, dancing and yodelling as an accompaniment. Diners are usually expected to join in—so be prepared for an uproarious evening and not a quiet chat. Try the leberknödel soup, pork chop serbischesart, tafelspitz and Sachertorte to follow. *LD (Reserve) open to 23.00. Closed Sun, L Sat.* A.Ax.B.Dc. **££**.

Old Vienna
2 G 19

94 New Bond St W1. 01-629 8716. Lavishly decorated Austrian restaurant. Small dance floor but the accordianist and singer will serenade you at your table. Warm lively atmosphere in which to enjoy some first-class cooking. Large varied menu with over 20 specialties to choose from. Good wine list. *LD open to 23.00. Closed Sun, L Sat.* A.Ax.B.Dc. **££**.

Tiroler Hut

27 Westbourne Grove W2. 01-727 3981. Typical Tyrolean atmosphere, including waitresses in national dress. Dancing to Austrian tunes and yodelling entertainment. Competent cooking, reasonably priced. *D open to 24.00. Closed Mon.* A.Ax.B.Dc. **£.**

Wurst Max

75 Westbourne Grove W2. 01-229 3771. Not strictly a restaurant, more of a café take-away. But the selection of German sausages and salads is worth a mention. Look out for the blue and white awning on the corner of Galway Rd. *Open to 04.00.* **£.**

Yodelling Sausage   **1 G 5**

159 Earl's Court Rd SW5. 01-370 5107. Serves every variety of sausage you can think of! Bavarian style restaurant, black tables and plain white walls. Taped music. Knuckle of pork, sauerkraut, bratwurst. Also English and Continental dishes. Good selection of German beers. *L summer only. D open to 02.00.* **£.**

Greek, Turkish and Cypriot

Greek and Turkish food are very similar in style. Both use plenty of oil, herbs and spices such as coriander and cumin. Cypriot restaurants abound in London which combine the best of Greek and Turkish dishes. Many people have been disappointed with the food in Greece expecting similar fare to that served in Greek restaurants here. Shish kebab is one of the most popular kebabs—marinated with herbs and charcoal grilled. Doner Kebab is pieces of lamb pressed down onto a perpendicular spit, rotated in front of a high charcoal fire and sliced off as it cooks. These are served with pitta and salads. Turks will use more yoghurt in their cooking than the Greeks and will often cook kebabs in yoghurt sauce. They also prefer to use rice whereas the Greeks like the taste of wheat. Sweets are very sticky and sugary. Some of the most popular are bakclava, kaideifi—thin shredded pastry filled with nuts and honey. Mezzes are also popular. Served like hors d'oeuvres, they offer a selection of the dishes that are available on the menu.

To drink try the Turkish wine or Greek retsina—white wine stored in barrels to which resin has been added. Ouzo is a good aperitif made from aniseed, similar to Pernod.

Adana Kebab Centre

17 Colomb St SE10. 01-858 1913. This excellent Turkish restaurant in South London is always bustling with activity. Watch your food being cooked by the chef in true taverna style. Authentic Mediterranean flavours. Try their mezze, börek stuffed with cheese and parsley, chicken with lemon and bay leaves. Drink Turkish buzbag. *D (Reserve Fri & Sat) open to 24.00. Closed Sun.* Dc. **£.**

Anemos
2 F 22

34 Charlotte St W1. 01-636 2289/01-580 5907. If you feel like going Greek, this is the place to do it! Dance on the tables, smash plates in this lively restaurant. Music blares out from loudspeakers and the waiters sing and clap—good raucous atmosphere. Through all the apparent chaos your meal will appear. Typical Greek fare. Taramosalata, houmous, kebabs. Drink retsina or Cypriot wines. *LD (Reserve D) open to 24.00. Closed Sun.* **£.**

Ararat Restaurant

249 Camden High St NW1. 01-267 0319. Cosy Greek-Armenian restaurant. Soft lighting and a Mediterranean atmosphere. Typical variety of kebabs, excellent kleftiko, moussaka and dolmades. Armenian specialities include Lakmajoun—grilled spiced minced meat served on pitta—or Keyma kebabs. Cypriot and French wines. *LD (Reserve) open to 00.30. Closed Mon.* A.Ax.B.Dc. **£.**

Beoty's
5 J 22

79 St Martin's Lane WC2. 01-836 8768. Perfect for after-theatre dinner. Old-fashioned courtesy still exists in this comfortable restaurant on two floors. Best to stick to the Greek specialties rather than the French. Stuffed vine leaves, kalamarakia—squid cooked in its own ink with wine, fried scampi, moussaka. Usual sweet pastries or try their halva—nougat with pistachios. *LD open to 23.30. Closed Sun.* A.Ax.B.Dc. **££.**

Chagalayan Kebab House
86 Brent St NW4. 01-202 8575. Local residents come regularly to this kebab house. Food is well prepared and appetisingly presented. Taped music. Charcoaled kebabs, lamb on the bone, moussaka; salads are always fresh. *LD (Reserve weekends) open to 24.00. Closed L Sun.* A.Ax.B.Dc. **£.**

Cypriana Kebab House
2 G 22

11 Rathbone St W1. 01-636 1057. Slightly dearer than most of the Cypriot restaurants in this area. Small family-run concern. Green vines adorn the entrance. Greek taped music. Pictures and knick-knacks from Cyprus hang on the wall. Specialties are kleftiko, afelia, moussaka, dolmades. *LD open to 23.30. Closed Sun, L Sat.* B.Dc. **£.**

Four Lanterns
2 E 22

96 Cleveland St W1. 01-387 0704. Serves exceptionally good kebabs and moussaka. Fresh salads with firm tomatoes, aubergines and peppers—delicious with pitta. Varied selection of wines and retsina. Dance to taped music in the evenings. *LD open to 01.00. Closed L Sat, L Sun.* A.Ax.B.Dc. **£.**

Havajah
2 H 22

16 Bateman St W1. 01-437 4736. Old Soho restaurant with an unchanged and unsmart atmosphere. This is compensated by the attentive and friendly service of the waiters. Try their kleftiko, stifado, moussaka. For dessert try the bird's nest or kaideifi. Taped music. *LD (Reserve D) open to 23.30. Closed Sun, L Sat.* A.Ax.B.Dc. **££.**

Helepi 1, 2 & 3
(1) 18 Leinster Terrace W2. 01-723 4097   **1 B 11**
(2) El Gaucho Steak House
84 Queensway W2. 01-229 4320.   **1 B 11**
(3) 106 Queensway W2. 01-727 1970.   **1 A 11**
In a fashionable quarter for Greek restaurants. They offer a wide selection of middle eastern food, all of which is well prepared and appetisingly presented. Service is courteous and leisurely. The mezze can be very tasty—try the charcoal grilled prawns, taramosalata or kebabs and dolmas. *LD (Reserve) open to 01.00.* **£.**

Hellenic
2 E 19

30 Thayer St W1. 01-935 1257. Noisy, crowded restaurant on two floors. Waiters are friendly and helpful in explaining dishes. Bistro atmosphere. Specialities include fish kebabs, afelia and moussaka; good farmhouse Greek cooking. To follow loukomades. *LD (Reserve) open to 23.00. Closed Sun.* **£.**

Kalamaras

66 Inverness Mews W2. 01-727 9122.   **1 B 11**
76–78 Inverness Mews W2. 01-727 9122.   **1 B 11**

Relaxed and informal restaurants. It is much smaller at number 66, where the food is slightly less expensive and they have no wine licence. The other restaurant is more gaily decorated with Greek rugs and pottery. Live Greek bouzouki music is played in the evenings and more unusual food is served. Try their spanakotyropitas—paper thin pastry with spinach and cheese filling; tsirosalata—smoked strips of salted fish. Wide selection of lamb dishes. For dessert home-made bougatsa and baclava. Winter specialities are spit lamb and suckling pig. *D (Reserve) open to 24.00. Closed Sun.* A.Ax.B.Dc. **££**.

Kebab and Houmous 2 F 22
95 Charlotte St W1. 01-636 3144. Happy little restaurant. Good place for entertaining friends. Taped bouzouki music. Excellent taramosalata, houmous and kebabs. *LD open to 23.00. Closed Sun.* **£**.

Little Akropolis 2 F 22
10 Charlotte St W1. 01-636 8198. Well-prepared Greek specialities in this charming old-fashioned restaurant. Polite and attentive service. Some European dishes as well as Greek favourites. Specialities include avoglemono soup—chicken soup with an egg and lemon sauce, moussaka—one of the best in London. If you still have some room try their rose petal jam pancakes. Drink Corinth wine. *LD (Reserve) open to 22.30. Closed Sun, L Sat.* A.Ax.B.Cb.Dc. **££**.

Marmares
29 Clifton Rise, New Cross SE14. 01-692 7022. Worth the journey from central London. Authentic Turkish cooking. Everything cooked in an open kitchen. Pleasantly realistic murals and pictures of Turkey. Really fresh ingredients and good lamb. Mainly kebabs and grills. Good side dishes. Recorded music. *LD open to 24.00. Fri & Sat to 01.30. Closed Mon.* A.B. **£**.

Modhitis 3 A 25
83 Bayham St NW1. 01-485 7890. Authentic taverna restaurant. Shared tables make it an excellent place for starting up conversations. Always crowded and very popular with students. Dishes are Greek-Cypriot. Lamb casserole is the speciality cooked with aubergines, cauliflower, potatoes or courgettes; afelia can be very oily. Standard starters and sweets. *LD open to 24.00. Closed Sun.* **£**.

Mykonos Greek Taverna 2 H 22
17 Frith St W1. 01-437 3603. Bright and lively Soho restaurant filled with Greek paraphernalia. Much frequented by the film and advertising world. Well-known for their moussaka and lamb kebabs marinated and cooked on the grill with pimentos, tomatoes and

onions. Very tasty kleftiko. Ouzo, Greek wines and brandy. *LD open to 23.30. Closed L Sat.* A.Ax.B.Dc. £.

Nontas

16 Camden High St NW1. 01-387 4579. Attractive dark brown and beige decor in this small Greek restaurant. Advisable to book as it is nearly always full. Although the waiters are busy, the service is attentive. Try their delicious fish kebabs, moussaka or the Nontas Special—smoked sausage, dolmas and kebabs on a bed of wheat. If you are really hungry the mezze is one of the most reasonably priced in London—pickled mullet, fried squid and the usual mezze selection. Yoghurt and honey for dessert. *LD (Reserve D) open to 23.45. Closed Sun.* A.Dc. £.

Romantica Taverna Restaurant 1 A 10

12 Moscow Rd W2. 01-727 7112. Definitely for courting couples. Charming restaurant on two floors, decorated with skins, laces, copper and worry beads. Candlelight and atmospheric background music. Especially strong in sea food—king prawns, red mullet, lobster, octopus cooked in red wine. Tender meat dishes—kebabs, kleftiko and souvla. Fresh fruit all the year round. *LD (Reserve D) open to 01.00.* A.Ax.B.Cb.Dc. ££.

Salamis 4 L 4

204 Fulham Rd SW10. 01-352 9827. Comfortable and relaxing atmosphere. Friendly and helpful service. You are remembered on your return visit here. A selection of Greek and Mediterranean dishes. Try squid cooked in their own ink; stuffed aubergines. The Golden Finale—pancake stuffed with a soufflé mixture of cream cheese, sultanas, almonds and lemon topped with a Grand Marnier sauce. *LD (Reserve D) open to 24.00. Closed Sun.* A.Ax.B.Dc. £.

Sultan's Delight 3 E 32

301 Upper St N1. 01-226 8346. Alluring pictures of belly dancers on the walls, Turkish chandeliers and a special party room known as the 'Sultan's Love Nest' at the rear of the restaurant. Authentic Turkish cuisine. Donner kebabs served with yoghurt, shish kebabs, dolmas and moussaka. Good Turkish coffee to follow

and real Turkish delights. *LD open to 01.00. Closed L Sun.* A.Ax.B.Dc. **£.**

Tarabya
107 Loampit Vale SE13. 01-691 1503. Very popular among the local residents. Service is attentive and friendly. Typical carefree taverna atmosphere. Taped music. Excellent houmous, kofte kebab. For dessert try their home-made yoghurt with honey. *D open to 02.00.* B. **£.**

Ttokkos Kebab House   2 E 22
56 Maple St W1. 01-580 4819. Small family run restaurant, beside the Post Office Tower. In the summer you can eat out on the verandah, which is prettily decorated with plants and flowers. Basic Greek food. Kebabs and moussaka. *LD (Reserve D) open to 23.00. Closed Sun, L Sat.* A.Ax.B.Dc. **£.**

White Tower   2 G 22
1 Percy St W1. 01-636 8141. After you have read your way through a lengthy menu complete with full history and explanation of each dish; and after you have taken in the splendid Byronic portraits, the refined atmosphere of the street level dining room, begin the meal with feathery light taramosalata and pâté Diane. The Greek inspired main courses include moussaka and shashlik as well as plain roast duck. Fresh fruit salad and Turkish coffee to end the meal. An excellent wine list. Doorman will park your car for you. *LD (Reserve) open to 22.30. Closed Sat & Sun.* A.Ax.B.Dc. **£££.**

Hungarian

Paprika is used as a flavouring in many Hungarian dishes, usually accompanied with cream—fresh or sour, or a rich butter sauce—chicken paprikash or goulash; pörrkölt—national onion stew; stuffed peppers; beef Esterhazy; letscho—a tasty vegetable mixture of peppers, tomatoes and onions. There are many other sauces that give a Hungarian accent to a dish—caper and dill sauce for fish; and carp, jellied or marinated, is a favourite. Or sweet-sour apples with cabbage, or a lemon-wine sauce with tripe. Nuts are also used inventively: chestnuts with cabbage or walnuts ground with sugar over noodles. Desserts are very rich and include the speciality Dobosh torte—thin slices of sponge with thick chocolate filling topped with caramel.

Csarda
2 F 22

74 Charlotte St W1. 01-580 7719. Brightly decorated, pictures of Hungary on the walls create a pleasing atmosphere. Deep fried mushrooms, beef goulash, veal Bakony, chicken paprika, gypsy steak—fillet steak in sour cream. Walnut pancakes to follow. Live music every evening. *LD (Reserve Fri & Sat) open to 02.00. Closed Sun.* A.Ax.B.Dc. **££**.

Gay Hussar
2 H 22

2 Greek St W1. 01-437 0973. Intimate, cosy, much-loved Soho restaurant with a loyal, rather sophisticated following. Try the stuffed cabbage, chilled wild cherry soup, pike with beetroot sauce, roast saddle of carp, goulash. To follow, orange curd pancakes or berries with whipped cream. Helpful service. Varied wine list. Essential to book. *LD (Reserve) open to 23.30. Closed Sun.* **££**.

Le Mignon
1 A 11

2 Queensway W2. 01-229 0093. Cheerful, lively atmosphere in which to enjoy some typical Hungarian cooking. Live gipsy orchestra. House sulz, chicken with paprika, fantanyeros, goulash. *LD open to 24.00. Closed Mon.* A.Ax.B.Dc. **££**.

Indian and Pakistani

The farther south in India you travel, the hotter the spices. Madras, Bendi and Vindaloo mean climbing degrees of heat. There is however no particular virtue in an excess of hotness—many people enjoy (and prefer) the more delicate flavour of a milder curry. Hindu cooking uses vegetables in rich liquid juices; Muslims use more meat and the food is drier. The best cooking is prepared in the traditional mud oven; spices are added individually to each dish, giving a distinctive and piquant flavour.

Agra
2 E 22

135 Whitfield St W1. 01-387 4828. Very popular and crowded restaurant. Don't expect a table to yourself; the friendly atmosphere makes up for any inconvenience. The waiters, although rushed, try to be as helpful as possible. Specialises in tandoori rather than curry dishes; all are freshly prepared and very tasty. *LD open to 24.00. Fri & Sat to 21.00.* A.Ax.B.Dc. **£.**

Anarkali

303 King St W6. 01-748 1760. A corner of India can be found in this very popular Hammersmith haunt; walls are covered with batik and paintings of Indian legends; the taped sitar music is not too loud. Subdued lighting. Food is quite strongly spiced. Tandoori dishes are well cooked and attractively presented: chicken dhansak, rogan gosht and if you want something mild try the prawn patia. *LD (Reserve D) open to 24.00.* A.Ax.B.Dc. **££.**

Asia Grill
1 A 8

26 Pembridge Rd W11. 01-727 5868. Unostentatious restaurant close to the Portobello Rd. Large selection of curries ranging from very mild to extra hot. *LD open to 24.00.* A.Ax.B.Dc. **£.**

Bangla Desh
2 C 18

52 Dorset St W1. 01-486 1135. Small, unpretentious restaurant that sustains a high, fully deserved local reputation. Begin with a meat or vegetable samosa and follow with chicken or prawn dhansak, meat masala, chicken vindaloo, various biryanis dishes all served with pualo rice. The tandoori chicken is also worth sampling, the nan and onion bhajees exceptional. Service is discreet and attentive. Coffee liberally poured. Food can also be taken away. *LD open to 23.30. Closed Sun.* B. **£.**

Bombay

2 Elm Terrace, Constantine Rd NW3. 01-485 9921. Skilful use of spices and good raw materials. Primarily a tandoori restaurant. Unlicensed but you are welcome to bring your own wine. Chicken and mushroom biryanis, methi gosht, aubergine and onion bhajee. *LD open to 23.00.* A.Ax.B.Dc. **£.**

Bullock Cart
77 Heath St NW3. 01-435 3602. Small, attractive Indian restaurant decorated with authentic Indian knick knacks. Tables well spaced and seating is comfortable. Plenty of hot curries—so be warned. A selection of tandoori and vegetable dishes. *LD open to 24.00. Closed L Mon.* A.Ax.B.Cb.Dc. **£.**

Curry House
756 Finchley Rd, Temple Fortune NW11. 01-458 6163. Small, local restaurant. An Indian atmosphere prevails and the recorded sitar music is obviously enjoyed by both customers and waiters. Try either the shami or reshmee kebabs, spinach gosht, mushroom and capsicum bhajee. Chapatis are well made. *LD (Reserve D) open to 24.00.* Ax.B.Dc. **£.**

Diwan-I-Am   **2 E 22**
161 Whitfield St W1. 01-387 0293. Small and interesting restaurant, decorated to look like a cave. Very popular with pre-theatre diners. Try the thali—a selection of small side dishes: mutton moghlai, bhoona gosht, and the specialities—tandoori chicken and prawn bhoona. *LD (Reserve) open to 23.45.* A.Ax.B.Dc. **£.**

Ganges Two   **2 B 14**
101 Praed St W2. 01-723 4096. Small, simple, family-run restaurant. Offers a superb range of dishes. Try their fried giant prawns, or chicken tikka which has a sharp lemon flavour; satkora also cooked with lemon and oranges. *D (Reserve) open to 23.00. L Sat & Sun only. Closed Mon.* A.Ax.B.Dc. **£.**

Gaylord   **2 F 21**
79 Mortimer St W1. 01-636 0808. Modern Indian abstract mural on the wall. Authentic Indian food prepared here and appetisingly presented. Tandoori chicken, lentils with sour cream, fried meat balls served in a curried sauce. Interesting Indian sweetmeats to follow. *LD open to 23.30.* A.Ax.B.Dc. **££.**

Gaylord Mayfair   **2 I 19**
16 Albemarle St W1. 01-629 9802. Opulently decorated restaurant. On the wall a mural of painted beads. Authentic and very well cooked food from the Kashmir region of India where the flavours are milder.

Try the khasta roti bread; goshtaba—meat balls of shredded lamb in spices fried in butter; also try their fried ball of cream cheese with a curry and cream sauce. *LD open to 23.30*. A.Ax.B.Dc. **££**.

Geetanjli 2 G 18
23 Brook St W1. 01-493 1779. Sikh restaurant with decor reminiscent of a rajah's palace, with plants and flowers, paintings of India on the wall. A huge stuffed lion greets you with bared teeth at the door. Chara masala, lamb pasanda, kulfi and shaslik. Of particular note among the house specialities is the tandoori pheasant and lobster. Worth trying the Indian tea flavoured with cloves and cardamom. *LD (Reserve) open to 23.00. Sun to 22.30*. A.Ax.B.Cb.Dc. **££**.

Goan Restaurant 3 C 28
16 York Way N1. 01-837 7517. Don't be daunted by the unpromising exterior and the rather cramped conditions inside. All the food is home-cooked. Authentic Goan dishes. Service is slow but the food when it arrives is worth waiting for. Goan specialities include sweetbreads and a prawn curry; nans are delicious. Drink wine or lassi with your meal. *LD open to 24.00. Closed Sun*. A.Ax.B.Dc. **£**.

Indira 2 D 16
62 Seymour St W1. 01-402 6733. Beautifully decorated Indian restaurant, close to Marble Arch. A good selection of vegetarian dishes: lentils, bhindi, dal tarka as well as traditional meat curries. Drink lassi with yoghurt. *LD (Reserve D) open to 23.15*. A.Ax.B.Dc. **££**.

Jamshid 1 I 19
6 Glendower Place SW7. 01-584 2309. One of the few places in London where you can sample genuine Parsee dishes. Decor is rather dowdy but the standard of food is excellent. Try the chicken or lamb dhansak, Parsee kebab, basmati rice. *LD open to 23.30. Closed Sun*. A.Ax.B.Cb.Dc. **£**.

Khan's
14 Westbourne Grove W2. 01-727 5420. Vast, plain whitewashed room with oriental arches and a bar in one corner. Bluish lights focus on the widely spaced tables and the overall impression, as seen through the large

windows from the street, is somewhat surreal. The specialities include tandoori bot kebab; kofti dilruba—spiced curried meat balls with a fresh cream and herb sauce; matter paneer—home-made white cheese with peas and herbs. Also a selection of vegetable dishes. *LD (Reserve D) open to 24.00.* A.Ax.B.Cb.Dc. **£.**

Kundan   5 O 18
3 Horseferry Rd SW1. 01-834 3434. A popular haunt with MPs and government officials. Very lavishly decorated basement restaurant in matching browns. Succulent tandoori dishes include tikha kebab, karahi kebab, charcoal grilled king prawns and seekh kebab zafrani. *LD (Reserve D) open to 24.00. Closed Sun.* A.Ax.B.Dc. **££.**

Light of India   4 K 5
276 Fulham Rd SW10. 01-352 5416. Special Moghlai dishes such as murgh massalum, khurzi chicken and lamb. Must order a day in advance. Also good tandoori dishes. Staff are willing to show you the clay ovens. *LD (Reserve) open to 24.00.* A.Ax.B.Cb.Dc. **£.**

Light of India   2 A 18
59 Park Rd NW1. 01-723 6753. Specialises in curry dishes. Pleasant and roomy. Malay curry, mutton khorma, Madras chicken. *LD (Reserve Sat & Sun) open to 23.30.* A.Ax.B.Dc. **£.**

Light of Nepal
268 King St W6. 01-748 3586. Extremely good Hammersmith restaurant, worth a special visit if you want an excellent meal without having to pay West End prices. Pleasingly decorated in browns and reds. Large helpings of tandoori chicken, tarka dhal, samosas, prawn patia, mutton Madras, dry bhindi. *LD open to 24.00.* A.Ax.B.Dc. **£.**

Maharani
27–29 Westbourne Grove W2. 01-727 5154. Courteous and pleasant restaurant. Well-presented food including two or three Nepalese dishes. Try the lamb Mughali which is excellent. Usual variety of accompaniments. *LD open to 24.00.* A.Ax.B.Dc. **£.**

Meghna Grill
219 High Rd, South Woodford E18. 01-504 0923. A

godsend if you happen to want a pick-me-up from the traffic queues on the North Circular or A11. A star in suburbia! Excellent dhal soup, bhoonas, tikkas and vindaloos, Special kurshi chicken must be ordered a day in advance. *LD open to 24.00*. Ax.B.Dc. **££.**

Mumtaz 2 A 18
4–10 Park Rd NW1. 01-723 0549. One of the most lavishly decorated Indian restaurants in town. Palms surround a pool on the patio. Inside there are gold filigree lampshades and the walls are painted white and red. Courteous service. Great wealth of side dishes. Buffet lunches and dinners on Sundays. Bombay duck, seekh kebab. Mumtaz pasinda, tandoori chicken. *LD open to 23.15*. A.Ax.B.Dc. **££.**

Naraine   **1 G 5**
10 Kenway Rd SW5. 01-370 3853. Sophisticated
restaurant which is very popular with local residents.
Indian decor. Friendly and attentive service. Fresh raw
materials are used. Mainly tandoori and curry dishes.
Tandoori chicken, rogan gosht, Bombay curry,
Bangalore curry. Gulayam for dessert. *LD open to
23.45* A.B.Dc. **£.**

Paramount   **1 I 7**
163 Old Brompton Rd SW5. 01-373 2817. Usual
Indian decor in this charming small restaurant. Service
is very friendly and also efficient. All the food is well
prepared and appetisingly presented. The menu is
typical of many other Indian restaurants but it is well
worth a visit if you are in the area. Rogan gosht,
chicken tikka and delicious chappatis. They are also
licensed. *D open to 00.45.* A.Ax.B.Dc. **£.**

Salloo's   **2 I 14**
62 Kinnerton St SW1. 01-235 4444. Luxurious oriental
decor to match the excellent standard of authentic
Pakistani cooking. Housed in a classy Belgravia mews,
with a bar-lounge on the ground floor and restaurant
upstairs. Some original dishes from the era of the Mogul
emperors. Haleem akbari, chicken jalfrezi, bataire
masala (quail), chicken in cheese, lamb barra, tandooris
and curries. *LD open to 23.30. Closed Sun.* A.Ax.B.Dc.
££.

Shezan   **2 I 12**
16–22 Cheval Place SW7. 01-589 7918. Justly
acclaimed since its opening for the excellence of its
Pakistani cooking, this cooly decorated basement
remains as good as ever (cool too in summer, thanks to
air conditioning). Try the tandoori favourite Murgh
Tikka Lahori; beef, lamb, chicken and vegetable
kebabs, curries or the lamb and chicken specialities. All
are prepared with singular delicacy. Nans are good,
vegetables, especially lentils and a chick pea dish—
kabuli chana, excellent, and the Basmati rice a
revelation. Oriental milk puddings topped with silver
leaf provide a decorative and refreshing conclusion.
Service is courteous, but sometimes slow. *LD (Reserve
D) open to 23.30. Closed Sun.* A.Ax.B.Cb.Dc. **££.**

Standard

23 Westbourne Grove W2. 01-727 4818. Below standard prices and above standard cooking. Occasional queues despite spacious seating. A menu of over 80 specialities including tandoori and vegetarian dishes. The fish masala, relatively rare in London restaurants, is excellent. Many Indian breads such as nan and stuffed paratha are also recommended. The mixed grill of tandoori specialities is quite delicious. For dessert try the kulfi—a cone filled with spices and ice-cream. *LD (Reserve) open to 24.00.* A.Ax.B. **£.**

Star of India   **1 I 7**

154 Old Brompton Rd SW5. 01-373 2901. Excellent Indian food and good service. Unsmart in a sophisticated neighbourhood. Mughlai dishes must be ordered a day in advance. Prawns biryani, kebabs. *LD open to 24.00. Sun to 23.30.* **£.**

Tandoori   **4 J 10**

153 Fulham Rd SW3. 01-589 7749. Pleasant decor with soft music. Sit back and relax at tables around the bar while you decide on your meal. Cooking is of a very high standard, using the traditional clay ovens. The lamb and chicken are carefully marinated with herbs and spices before cooking. Tandoori chicken or lamb, rogan gosht, fish curry. *D (Reserve) open to 00.30. Sun L to 15.00.* A.Ax.B.Cb.Dc. **££.**

Tandoori of Mayfair   **2 I 17**

37a Curzon St W1. 01-629 0600. Charming and elegant restaurant. Beautifully decorated with hanging curtains, subdued lighting and attractive sculpture. Service is attentive and all the dishes are carefully explained. Courteous manager, who will be pleased to show the kitchen to you. Kababe murgh tikka—diced chicken cooked in yoghurt and then barbecued: jhinga tandoori—giant prawns seasoned with spices and cooked over charcoal: matte panir—soft cheese cooked with peas in a curry sauce. Delicious kulfi for dessert. *LD open to 00.30. Closed Sun.* A.Ax.B.Cb.Dc. **££.**

Tandoor Mahal   **2 D 22**

321 Euston Rd NW1. 01-387 2995. Unpretentious Indian establishment, offering good food if you are near

Euston or King's Cross Station. Generous portions, without spending too much. Tandoori dishes, choice of curries and biryanis. *LD open to 24.00*. A.Ax.Dc. **£**.

Veeraswamy's   **2 I** 20
99–101 Regent St (Entrance in Swallow St) W1. 01-734 1401. Atmosphere of a pre-war Indian club. Greeted by a turbaned doorman. Colonial style decor, the curries are not overspiced. Traditionally dressed waiters attend you. Large choice of curries, kebabs and well-prepared rice dishes. *LD open to 23.30. Sun to 22.00*. A.Ax.B.Cb.Dc. **££**.

Viceroy of India   **2 A** 18
3 Glentworth St NW1. 01-486 3401. Large and elegant with fountains in the foyer and dining area. Appetising Indian cooking and many well executed tandoori specialities. Skilful use of spices and herbs. Try tandoori chicken or prawns, boti kebab, rumali roti. Several varieties of nan including one stuffed with onion bulcha. Polite service. *LD open to 23.30*. A.Ax.B.Dc. **££**.

Volga   **2 E** 22
45 Grafton Way W1. 01-387 2107. Dim lighting and Indian works of art add interest to this family owned restaurant. Service is helpful and attentive. All dishes are carefully explained. Lamb's brains Pakora, samosa, shiekh kebab; silver topped kusmalia makes a lovely sweet. Very cheap set L. *LD open to 23.45*. A.Ax.B.Cb.Dc. **£**.

Inexpensive eating

Places where you can eat for around £4.00 or under. The café serving 'sausage, egg and chips' is not included here, however excellent some may be. This list includes all styles of cooking and prizes a distinctive atmosphere and good value for money. See also under 'American', 'Chinese', 'Indian and Pakistani', 'Italian', 'Greek, Turkish and Cypriot' and 'Vegetarian & Wholefood' sections for restaurants serving cheaper meals.

Alpino Restaurants
42 Marylebone High St W1. 01-935 4640.   **2 D** 19

29 Leicester Square WC2. 01-839 2939.　　　**5 J** 22
102 Wigmore St W1. 01-935 4181.　　　　　**2 E** 18
154 Gloucester Rd SW7. 01-370 5625.　　　**1 I**　7
Pleasing Italian atmosphere in these alpine-style restaurants. Busy and crowded at all times. Service is quick and efficient. Generous portions of pasta or try some of their veal or chicken dishes. *LD open to 23.30. Closed Sun.* A.Ax.B.Dc. **£.**

Al Ristoro　　　　　　　　　　　　　**1 B** 8

205 Kensington Church St W8. 01-727 3184. Near Notting Hill Gate this friendly and relaxed restaurant is well worth a visit. Genuine and tasty Italian food available. Try their hors d'oeuvres, cannelloni, saltimbocca Romana with Italian ices to follow. *LD open to 23.30. Closed L Sun.* **£.**

Ark　　　　　　　　　　　　　　　　**1 C** 9

122 Palace Gardens Terrace W8. 01-229 4024. Good French provincial food. Dishes are chalked up on a board. Menu is changed regularly. They also offer a variety of international dishes. There is a more expensive version of 'Ark' in Kensington High Street. *LD (Reserve) open to 23.30. Closed L Sun.* Ax.B. **£.**

D'Artagnan　　　　　　　　　　　　**2 D** 18

19 Blandford St W1. 01-935 1023. Small intimate and wood panelled. Simple French food at a very reasonable cost. Menu varies according to season. If the following are on the menu they are well worth trying; artichauts San Marlo, deep fried mushrooms, scaloppine de veau d'Artagnan. To follow profiteroles, crème caramel, fresh fruit or fruit flans. *LD open to 22.30. Closed Sat & Sun.* A.B. **£.**

Asterix　　　　　　　　　　　　　　**4 L** 11

329 King's Rd SW3. 01-352 3891. Brick walls and wooden chairs. Soothing classical music. Typical Breton 'crêperie'. Sweet or savoury filled pancakes in lots of combinations. Prawns and tomatoes; cheese, sliced ham and tomato: cheese and asparagus; honey and lemon. *LD open to 24.00.* **£.**

Le Bistingo

5 Trebeck St W1. 01-499 3292.　　　　　**2 I** 17
3 Lower Grosvenor Place SW1. 01-834 0722.　**5 K** 16

7 Kensington High St W8. 01-937 0932.	**1 D** 4
56 Old Brompton Rd SW7. 01-589 1929.	**1 I** 7
57 Old Compton St W1. 01-437 0784.	**2 I** 22
43 New Oxford St WC2. 01-836 1011.	**3 H** 23
65 Fleet St EC4. 01-353 4436.	**6 K** 26
117 Queensway W2. 01-727 0743.	**1 A** 11
332/334 King's Rd SW3. 01-352 4071.	**4 L** 4

Excellent value bistros serving provincial French cooking, with English undertones. Menu is chalked up on a blackboard. Good dishes of the day. Fresh sardines, scampi, venison, bananas au rhum. Carafes. Most of the branches have the same opening times. *LD open to 23.00.* A.Ax.B.Cb.Dc. **£.**

Bistro Vino

1 Old Brompton Rd SW7. 01-589 3888.	**1 I** 9
303 Brompton Rd SW3. 01-589 7898.	**4 J** 10
5 Clareville St SW7. 01-373 3903.	**1 I** 8
2 Hollywood Rd SW10. 01-352 6439.	**4 K** 6

A 'chain' of separately managed but similar style informal restaurants. Subdued lighting and closely packed tables helps to create a bistro atmosphere. Popular among young people. Various starters; onion soup is always well worth trying. To follow peppered or garlic steak, chicken chasseur. Limited selection of sweets. Licensed. *D open to 23.45.* **£.**

Casserole
3 G 23

67 Tottenham Court Rd W1. 01-636 1099. A basement room with good dishes served by helpful and attentive waitresses. Quick service. Omelettes, roast meats, boeuf bourguignonne, various salads. To follow trifle, gâteaux, home-made apple pie, sorbet. Breakfast is also served at weekends. *LD open to 24.00. Sun to 23.00.* **£.**

Ceylon Tea Centre
2 H 20

22 Regent St W1. 01-930 8632. Suitable atmosphere for enjoying a decent cup of tea near Piccadilly Circus. Varied and interesting selection of salads, savouries and cheese flans. *L open to 18.00. Closed Sun.* **£.**

Chelsea Kitchen
4 L 10

98 King's Rd SW3. 01-589 1330. Part of the Stockpot group and also the most popular of the chain. Always full of young people drifting in from the King's Rd. Healthy portions of moussaka, goulash or spaghetti. To

follow ice-cream and hot chocolate sauce. Licensed.
LD open to 23.45. **£.**

Costas Grill 1 B 8
14 Hillgate St W8. 01-229 3794. Good Greek meal of
avgolemono (lemon, chicken and egg soup), and steak
stewed in wine at a reasonable price. Eat outdoors in
summer. *LD open to 22.30. Closed Sun.* **£.**

Crêperie 2 F 19
56a South Molton St W1. 01-629 4794. Cool white and
green decor makes a refreshing escape from the bustle
of Oxford St. Delicious Breton pancakes made of
buckwheat are served here. Try them stuffed with
spinach, egg and cheese or ratatouille. A simple lemon
and sugar pancake to follow makes a satisfying meal.
Wine by the glass. *LD open to 24.00. Closed Sun.* **£.**

Daquise 1 I 9
20 Thurloe St SW7. 01-589 6117. Very popular with
Polish emigrés, this restaurant serves simple,
inexpensive but very well prepared dishes. Borscht,
stuffed cabbage, bigor and sausages, shaslik. Also open
for morning coffee and afternoon tea when they serve
some of the most delicious pastries in London. *LD open
to 23.35.* **£.**

The Granary 2 I 19
39 Albemarle St W1. 01-493 2978. Busy self-service
restaurant on two levels. Fresh and lively atmosphere,
plenty of asparagus ferns, plain brick walls and pine
furnishing. Daily dishes may include lamb and mint
casserole, lemon chicken, moussaka, hot avocado pear
with spinach, prawns and cheese, salad niçoise, curried
chicken salad, ratatouille, some vegetarian quiches and
various mixed salads. Extensive range of desserts—
gâteaux, lemon soufflé, Austrian coffee cake, mousses
and strawberry japonnaise. Wine by the glass, lagers
and fresh fruit juices. *L open to 18.50. Sat to 14.30.
Closed Sun.* **£.**

Hamburger Products 2 I 21
1 Brewer St W1. 01-437 7119. This is a snack bar
behind a fish store. Cockney atmosphere in the
tradition of the 19th century fish parlour. Fish freshly
caught and home-smoked. Smoked eel with pepper

salad. Trout with beetroot salad. *L open to 15.00.
Closed Sat & Sun.* **£.**

India Club   **6 K 23**
143 Strand WC2. 01-836 0650. Founded by Krishna
Menon. This down-at-heel canteen is very popular
among students. The curries are pedestrian, but
generous portions attract the hungry. But there are
some South Indian specialities which are well worth
trying. Sambar, masala dosai, dahi vada. *LD open to
22.00. Sun to 21.00.* A.Ax.B.Dc. **£.**

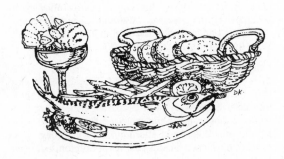

La Jardinière   **1 A 5**
148 Holland Park Avenue W11. 01-221 6090. On two
floors, charming French restaurant with attractive
hanging plants adorning the rooms. The menu changes
monthly. Stuffed mushrooms with mince, garlic and
herbs; confit de canard. To follow crêpes or tarte aux
pommes. Taped French music. *D (Reserve) open to
23.45. L Sun to 14.30. Closed Mon.* Ax.B. **£.**

Jimmy's   **2 H 22**
23 Frith St W1. 01-437 9521. This restaurant has
managed to retain its bohemian atmosphere, despite
changing fashions. Crumbs on the floor, unkempt
waiters, empty bottles—but nearly everyone loves it.
Huge helpings of Cypriot food at very reasonable
prices. Specialities include beef stew, moussaka, lamb
tava, aphelia or pastuchi. To follow baklava or kateifi,
two very popular though sticky sweets. *LD open to
22.30. Closed Sun.* **£.**

Justin de Blank   **2 E** 18
54 Duke St W1. 01-629 3174. Attractive cool and leafy
self-service restaurant. Expect to queue at lunchtime.
Food is well-prepared and appetisingly presented. Their
bread is all home-made. Lebanese cucumber and mint
soup for starters—very refreshing in summer. Pâtés,
quiches, savoury pies. Try their fruit brûlée for dessert.
LD open to 21.30. Closed Sun, D Sat. **£.**

Justin de Blank at the ICA   **5 K** 20
Nash House, The Mall SW1. 01-839 6762. Meal with a
difference in this arts complex in the Mall. Split level
dining area. If you are not in a rush you can while away
many hours just chatting to friends, or spend time
looking at the art exhibition before eating. Food is
mainly vegetarian—lasagne with courgettes, tomatoes,
onions and cheese sauce. Salads are always fresh. *LD
open to 20.45. Closed Mon. (M at the door)* **£.**

Khyber Pass   **1 I** 9
21 Bute St SW7. 01-589 7311. Particularly good
inexpensive Indian eating house. Clean and quiet with
polite and enthusiastic service. Kebabs, prawn patia,
chicken vindaloo. Licensed for wine or lager. *LD open
to 23.30.* A.Ax.B.Dc. **£.**

King's Road Jam   **4 L** 7
289a King's Rd SW3. 01-352 5390. Agile young people
are attracted to this restaurant. Tables are built in
alcoves on different levels of scaffolding which people
have to climb. Choose how bright or dim you want the
lighting; the volume of the music is also your own
choice. The set meals are very reasonably priced.
Smoked mackerel, egg mayonnaise, steaks, duck, pork,
chilli con carne. For desserts try their profiteroles. Also
a vegetarian menu. *D open to 23.30.* A.B. **£.**

Macarthurs
147 Church Rd SW13. 01-748 3630.
248 Upper Richmond Rd West SW14. 01-876 4445.
Lively local hamburger joints. Bright red wooden
tables, plants, paintings and taped music. Steaks,
hamburgers with various toppings, chef's special salad,
home-made brownies and milk shakes. The waitresses
wear peaked caps with flashing lights in the evening. *LD
open to 23.30.* **£.**

Mildreds   1 D 8
135 Kensington Church St W8. 01-727 5452. Friendly
restaurant usually exhibiting paintings. Good value
pies, quiches, pâtés, beef bourguignonne, chicken
dishes and a more expensive sirloin steak with Stilton.
Fresh vegetables. Delicious cheesecake, apple tart and
chocolate mousse. Wine bar in the front. *LD open to
22.30. Closed Sun.* **££.**

Mille Pini   3 H 25
33 Boswell St WC1. 01-242 2434. Popular Italian
trattoria patronised by staff from the Italian hospital.
Although the service is friendly, it can be very rushed on
occasions. Try their pastas, pizza Mille Pini, pollo
sopresso or their veal dishes. The house carafe is
reasonable. *LD (Reserve D) open to 23.00. Closed Sun.
Children.* **£.**

Mustoe Bistro
73 Regent's Park Rd NW1. 01-586 0901. Small,
candle-lit bistro which has long been popular with the
residents of Primrose Hill. Not the best cooked food in
London, but the prices are competitive. Advisable to
book for two, as you might have to share. For starters
aubergine and yoghurt, or curried eggs; garlic or pepper
steak to follow. Good sweets trolley. *LD (Reserve) open
to 23.15. Sun to 22.45. Closed Mon. L weekdays.* **£.**

My Old Dutch
132 High Holborn WC1. 01-404 5008.   3 I 23
36 Dover St W1. 01-499 4316.   2 I 19
Traditional Dutch farmhouse decor, pine tables and
chairs, walls lined with prints of Dutch masters. More
than one hundred varieties of sweet and savoury
pancakes, large in size and very good value. Licensed.
Ample seating and waitress service. *LD open to 24.00.
Thur, Fri & Sat to 01.00.* **£.**

New Kebab House   2 F 22
12 & 14 Charlotte St W1. 01-580 1049. Spartan Greek-
Cypriot restaurant, with records playing Greek songs.
Service is leisurely—it leaves you with plenty of time
for chatting with friends in true taverna style. Small
menu of taramosalata, houmous, pork or lamb kebabs.
Retsina, Cypriot wines or ouzo are suitable
accompaniments. *LD open to 24.00. Closed Sun.* **£.**

Nineteen 4 J 11

19 Mossop St SW3. 01-589 4971. Very popular with the young; many come after a Chelsea drinks party in large groups (usually rather merry ones). Bistro atmosphere with scrubbed tables and candles. Food consistently good value. Veal and kidney Stroganoff, chicken Kiev, steaks, veal escalope. Licensed. *D open to 23.45.* **£.**

Obelix

294 Westbourne Grove W11. 01-229 1877. Friendly crêperie decorated with cartoons of Asterix and Obelix. Adults may relax with newspapers in the French style, while books are available for children. Choice sweet crêpes with wide-ranging fillings. Black cherries and ice cream or bananas in rum are two favourites. Also savoury buckwheat galettes and more substantial specialities marked up on a blackboard. Good selection of real ciders. Taped music. *LD open to 23.00.* **£.**

Pasticceria Amalfi 2 J 22

31 Old Compton St W1. 01-437 7284. Lively and crowded Italian restaurant in Soho. Excellent veal, chicken and home-made pasta dishes. All pastries are delicious but their choux pastry filled with sweet cheese and cream is excellent. Cheeses imported straight from Italy. *LD 23.30.* A.B.Dc. **£.**

Pizza Express

30 Coptic St WC1. 01-636 2244.	3 H 24
363 Fulham Rd SW10. 01-352 5300.	4 K 6
15 Gloucester Rd SW7. 01-584 9078.	1 F 8
29 Wardour St W1. 01-434 1620.	2 I 21
137 Notting Hill Gate W11. 01-229 60000.	1 A 8
10 Dean St W1. 01-437 9595.	2 H 22
189 New Kings Rd SW6. 01-736 1145.	4 L 4
26 Porchester Gdns W2. 01-229 7784.	1 A 10

High St chain of restaurants to be found in and around London. Decor is mainly red and white. The pizza ovens are usually strategically placed, for those interested in watching their pizzas being cooked. The dough is light. Wine by the glass. Good fresh fruit salad and ice-creams. *LD open to 24.00.* **£.**

Pizza House 2 F 22

54 Goodge St W1. 01-636 9590. Lively, bustling and

crowded pizza house. Quick and attentive service on both floors. Excellent pizzas, pastas and meat dishes. Typical Italian desserts such as zabaglione or ice-cream. *LD open to 23.00. Closed Sun.* £.

Plexis   2 E 18
1c St Christopher's Place W1. 01-935 1047. Behind Oxford St, this is the ideal spot for exhausted shoppers. The menu is varied, but try their speciality Chicken Plexis—chicken served on a bed of rice covered in cheese and a cream and mushroom sauce. Licensed. *LD open to 22.45. Closed Sun.* £.

Pooh Corner   4 R 8
246 Battersea Park Rd SW11. 01-228 9609 Unassuming façade, leads into the world of Winnie the Pooh. Just over the river from Chelsea, this restaurant is very popular among young people. The menu is frequently changed and quite unintelligible, but the waitresses are very good at explaining what is available—A Leek in Bed, Piglet Wounded Knee, Zorbas Lament. Generous quantities of well cooked food. Essential to book. Set price. *D open to 23.00. Closed Sun.* £.

Porters   6 J 23
17 Henrietta St WC2. 01-836 6466. Large, pillared dining room lined with colourful modern paintings. Imaginative, good value, traditional English fare: cockie leekie soup, savoury spinach roundels, ramekin of meats. Various pies with delicious fillings, spiced pot roasted beef in ale, chicken with forcemeat in poachers sauce. Real English puddings or potted Stilton. *LD open to 23.30.* A.B. £.

Ristorante Italiano   2 H 18
54 Curzon St W1. 01-629 2742. Bargain food in Mayfair. An upstairs, downstairs restaurant without pretension and a genuine Italian flavour. The dishes are not superb but extremely good at the price. Carafe wines. Helpful service. Pastas, scaloppine al marsala, osso buco. Handy for the Curzon cinema. *LD open to 23.35. Closed Sun.* £.

Ristorante da Sandro   3 H 25
Tavola Calda, 3 Liverpool Victorian House, 3–4 Southampton Row WC1. 01-405 6658. Very good self-

service Italian dishes. Appetising cold fish and meat dishes and salads. Also hot lasagne, cannelloni and usually a meat dish of the day. Licensed. *LD open to 23.15. Closed Sun.* £.

Seashell Fish Bar 2 A 17
35 Lisson Grove NW1. 01-723 8703. Would make an interesting, if unconventional, change of atmosphere from watching cricket at Lords. Reputedly one of the best fish and chip shops in London. The menu offers 14 different varieties of fish and explains that no fish can be offered that cannot be bought fresh. Hot crisp haddock and halibut. *LD open to 22.30. Closed Sun & Mon.* £.

Shah 3 C 23
124 Drummond St NW1. 01-387 1480. Small, local Indian restaurant in a delapidated area behind Euston. Popular with curry enthusiasts as they serve over eleven different chicken curries, all tasty and well prepared. If you go in a crowd try their Mogul dishes which are the speciality of the house. *LD open to 23.15.* £.

Spaghetti Houses
10 Blenheim St W1. 01-629 9894.	2 F 19
24 Cranbourn St WC2. 01-836 8168.	5 J 22
74 Duke St W1. 01-629 6097.	2 E 18
15–17 Goodge St W1. 01-636 6582.	2 F 22
20 Sicilian Avenue WC1. 01-405 5215.	3 H 25
77 Knightsbridge SW1. 01-235 8141.	2 I 14
4 Hans Rd SW3. 01-589 7364.	2 I 12
Vecchia Milano, Welbeck St W1. 01-935 2371.	2 E 19

Genuine Italian spaghetti houses, friendly and busy. Decorated with chianti bottles. Seating on the pavement in Sicilian Avenue. Service is quick and the food is always hot. Minestrone, pastas, gnocchi, saltimbocca alla Romana. To follow delicious pastries or ice-cream. Wine and espresso coffee. *LD open to 23.00. Closed Sun.* £.

Stage
63 Golders Green Rd NW11. 01-455 2256. Friendly family restaurant, colourfully decorated in shades of pink, brown and orange. Large menu with Jewish specialities: chopped liver, gefilte fish, salt beef, schmaltz herring and bagels. Also pastrami, veal and

some more expensive French dishes. An American bar for quick snacks and a good take-away delicatessen. *LD open to 24.00. Closed D Fri.* Ax.B.Dc. **£**.

Stockpot 2 I 13
6 Basil St SW3. 01-589 8627. Plain decor: white walls with pine tables and benches. Informal, noisy atmosphere which attracts the young. Home-made soups, casseroles and sweets at popular prices. Vegetables tend to be of the frozen variety. *LD open to 22.30. Closed Sun.* **£**.

Tango 3 J 23
38 Long Acre WC2. 01-836 7639. Unusual café-style restaurant offering North and South American dishes, as well as breakfast, coffee and cakes. Stripped pine floors, spacious seating and Argentinian prints. Steaks, hamburgers, chilli con carne, tortillas, tacos, buritos, crispy pancake rolls, Argentinian casserole and stuffed green peppers. Live music after 21.00. *LD open to 01.00.* A.Ax.B.Cb.Dc. **£**.

Toad Hall 4 O 7
64 Battersea Bridge Rd SW11. 01-228 8380. Run on similar lines to Pooh Corner, this restaurant is also very popular. Small patio at the back for pleasant summer eating. Menu is limited, but all the dishes are tasty and well cooked. Well worth a visit. Set price. *D (Reserve) open to 23.00. Closed Sun.* **£**.

Trattoria Aqualino 3 E 32
Camden Passage N1. 01-226 5454. A mixture of Turko-Italian food. Related to the more expensive Portofino next door. In a charming alley, tucked between antique shops; the site of the Camden Passage antiques market on Wed and Sat. Very simple restaurant. Pizzas, spare ribs, veal and chicken dishes, pastas, kebabs, good salads. *LD open to 23.00. Closed Sun.* **£**.

Tuttons 6 J 23
11–12 Russell St, Covent Garden WC2. 01-836 1167. Stark, spacious cream and pine interior with splashes of colour from red chairs. Taped music. Tables outside under awning. Serve breakfast; snacks—salads, quiches, pâtés and cheese; a full meal—whitebait,

steaks, plat du jour; or just a coffee. Varied wine list from next door Old Chelsea Wine Stores; the drinks licence is that of a pub. *LD open to 23.30. Sun to 22.30.* A.Ax.B.Dc. **£.**

Zia Teresa 2 I 12
6 Hans Rd SW3. 01-589 7634. Tends to be very crowded at lunchtime with Knightsbridge shoppers. Pleasing Italian restaurant with a good choice of dishes: gnocchi, pastas, veal and chicken. Wine sold by the glass, espresso coffee. *LD open to 23.45. Closed Sun.* **£.**

International

Many of the top class hotels have excellent restaurants with international cuisine, in particular the Savoy, Dorchester, Carlton Tower and the Connaught. We have also listed here those restaurants of merit that do not specialise in the food of any particular country, but pick from the best dishes of the world, frequently blending ingredients and flavours to provide some quite distinctive cooking.

Barque & Bite
Prince Albert Rd NW1. 01-485 8137. Converted barge on the Regent canal. The upper deck has the better view across the park. Standard menu of soups, escargots, salmon; guinea fowl served in an orange sauce; steaks and duck. For dessert fruit salad, fresh strawberries in season and gâteaux from the trolley. Varied wine list. *LD (Reserve) open to 23.30. Closed Sun, L Sat.* A.Ax.B.Cb.Dc. **££.**

Ben's of Westminster 5 M 17
29 Victoria St SW1. 01-222 0424. A parliamentary theme lends extra character to this attractive restaurant conveniently situated near the House of Commons. There is even a division bell in the main dining room to call MPs back to the House for an important vote. English and international menu includes steak Ruvin, suprême of chicken Westminster, smoked trout Britannia, Egg of the Yard (poached egg with smoked salmon and hollandaise sauce), Backbencher prawn. Good clarets. *LD (Reserve) open to 22.45. Closed Sun.* A.Ax.B.Dc. **££.**

Brompton Grill   **4 J 11**

243 Brompton Rd SW3. 01-589 2129. Unpretentious food of a high order served by loyal staff in pleasantly ungimmicky surroundings—old chandeliers, plush wallpaper and velvet seating. In the same hands for over 30 years; its devotees speak highly of it. Large international menu. Bisque de homard, tournedos Rossini, Scotch salmon, pasta, fine grills. Good special English set lunch. *LD (Reserve) open to 23.00. Sun to 22.30. Closed L Sat.* A.Ax.B.Cb.Dc. **££.**

Carlton Tower, Rib Room   **5 K 13**

Cadogan Place SW1. 01-235 5411. A cheerful restaurant, notable for its warm decor and Topolski drawings as well as the excellence of its beef. Roasts and grills, soups or smoked fish to start, apple pie to follow. Fine wine list, welcoming service and an accomplished barman are added advantages. The fixed price lunch menus offer good value. *LD open to 22.45. Sun to 22.15.* A.Ax.B.Cb.Dc. **£££.**

Carriers   **3 E 32**

2 Camden Passage N1. 01-226 5353. Conceived by the famous cookery writer Robert Carrier. Eat in either the pink room, a mirror room, or a lush, ivy covered Gothic greenhouse in the garden. Imaginative, ambitious table

d'hôte menu with the emphasis on rich cream sauces. Classic dishes include the lamb in Greek pastry, roulade of red caviar, petit pot au chocolat à l'orange. Service is attentive. Outstanding claret and burgundy. *LD (Reserve) open to 23.30. Closed Sun.* Ax. **£££**.

Chanterelle   1 I 6
119 Old Brompton Rd SW7. 01-373 7390. Attractive fresh decor in this crowded restaurant with new brighter lighting. Generous helpings of elaborate dishes, distinctive in style if somewhat rich for the digestion. Mousse of Stilton with Armagnac, trout marinated with white wine, orange and lemon are among the specialities. Set lunch and à la carte menu. Good value. *LD (Reserve) open to 24.00. Closed L Sun.* A.Ax.B.Dc. **££**.

Claridge's Causerie   2 G 18
Brook St W1. 01-629 8860. More intimate than the formal restaurant, this pretty and luxurious room offers a quite different menu. There is a list of English and French dishes, but the main interest is provided by a handsome and impeccably presented cold table. The diner's choice of drink in part determines the cost of the meal. Especially agreeable at lunchtime. *LD open to 23.30. Closed Sat.* A.Ax.B.Dc. **£££**.

Connaught Hotel   2 H 22
Carlos Place W1. 01-499 7070. Long pre-eminent with a reputation for outstanding cuisine, the splendid room with its panelling, mirrors and chandeliers remains a fit setting for dishes French and English, reliably prepared from fresh materials of the highest quality. Oeufs de cailles Maintenon, crêpes de volaille Florentine, oxtail, baron of lamb from the trolley, filet de boeuf en croûte, marvellous game, bread and butter pudding. Outstanding wine list, polished service. *LD open to 22.00. Grill Room closed Sat & Sun.* A. **£££**.

Dorchester Grill   2 H 16
Park Lane W1. 01-629 8888. Outstanding cuisine in magnificent surroundings—a Spanish setting in the grill. Cooking leans towards the French, but many fine British dishes are available, such as tender Scotch salmon, cooked to a turn. Faultless service. *LD open to 24.00.* A.Ax.B.Cb.Dc. **£££**.

Dukes Hotel Restaurant   **5 J 19**
35 St James's Place SW1. 01-491 4840. Small, refined
dining room decorated with antiques in a quiet hotel in a
cul-de-sac off St James's St. English and French
specialities which are often changed. The sweets are
particularly tempting—soufflé, cheesecake, mousse,
gâteau. Attentive service. Reasonable wine list. *LD
(Reserve) open to 22.00.* A.Ax.B.Cb.Dc. **£££.**

L'Epicure   **2 H 22**
28 Frith St W1. 01-437 2829. Confident, rather
flamboyant establishment. Good Franco-Italian
cooking marked by the freshness of all raw materials.
Note the chicken pancakes, the boeuf Stroganoff,
kidneys in marsala and scampi. Limited wine list. *LD
(Reserve L) open to 23.15. Closed Sun, L Sat.*
A.Ax.B.Dc. **££.**

Five Five Five
555 Battersea Park Rd SW11. 01-228 7011. A
welcome oasis in a district of mansion flats and
gasworks. A small brightly decorated restaurant
covered in posters and holiday mementos. Attentive
service. Well prepared, sometimes imaginative food in
large, not too expensive portions. Home-made chicken
and duck pâté, garlic sausage; to follow, pork
marinated in Calvados and cider, trout in dill and cream
sauce, lamb served with wine and herbs, garlic and
plum sauce. *D open to 24.00. Closed Sun & Mon.* **££.**

La Fontana   **5 M 12**
101 Pimlico Rd SW1. 01-730 6630. Discreet,
sophisticated restaurant hung with brightly coloured
rugs. Local following appreciate the well-prepared,
mainly French and Italian dishes. Good onion soup,
cannelloni, entrecôte poivré à la crème, osso buco.
Background music. *LD (Reserve D) open to 23.30.
Closed Sun, L Sat.* Ax.Dc. **££.**

Frederick's
Camden Passage N1. 01-359 2888. Originally a public
house, renamed after Prince Augustus Frederick.
Large, airy room tastefully decorated in cream and
brown, hung with portraits set off by some elaborate
dried flower arrangements. Try the deep fried
mushrooms, the bouché au fruits de mer, the bisque de

homard au Cognac. To follow, pork chops coated with cheese, mustard and cream, duck in peach sauce, lamb's kidneys sautéd in gin and juniper berries or one of the fortnightly specialities. Steadily popular at lunchtime. Now also a built-on garden room. Good selection of wines. *LD (Reserve) open to 23.30. Closed Sun.* A.Ax.B.Cb.Dc. **£££**.

Friends   **6 J** 24
30 Wellington St WC2. 01-836 5520. Victorian bric-a-brac, large mirrors and a bright wooden 'yellow brick road' running through the centre of the restaurant are details of decor well-suited to the sophisticated clientele, drawn from the theatrical and music world. The place is, in fact, owned by Elton John's manager. Mixture of French and English cuisine. For starters—poached egg in pastry with smoked haddock cream sauce, or soup of the day. Rack of lamb, sweetbreads and veal kidneys in white wine sauce, boneless rib of trout stuffed with spinach, shallots and mushrooms. Good fresh vegetables. Pianist and singer every evening. *LD (Reserve D) open to 24.00. Closed Sun, L Sat.* A.Ax.B.Dc. **££**.

Hyde Park Hotel, Cavalry Room   **2 H** 14
66 Knightsbridge SW1. 01-235 2000. Managed by Trust House Forte, who have taken pains to make it live up to its reputation. Agreeable, dignified panelled dining room, but without the splendid park view of the main restaurant. Mainly French and English dishes, all prepared from fresh raw materials. Good roasts from the trolley, oeufs en cocotte, filet de boeuf Lutèce. *LD (Reserve) open to 22.30. Closed Sat.* A.Ax.B.Cb.Dc. **££**.

Inigo Jones   **5 J** 22
14 Garrick St WC2. 01-836 6456. Extremely popular restaurant in a converted Victorian building, originally a workshop for the designing and making of stained glass. Brick walls, large stained glass windows and distinctive lighting create a truly romantic setting. Original menu is changed monthly. Fresh herring fillets with apple, onion, pickled cucumber and sour cream, grilled breast of duck with carrot and cauliflower purée, carré d'agneau en croûte, steak tartare. *LD (Reserve) open to 23.45. Closed Sun, L Sat.* A.Ax.B.Dc. **£££**.

Ivy 2 I 22
1 West St WC2. 01-836 4751. Old established, first-rate restaurant, popular with theatrical personalities. Deep velvet chairs and period paintings enhance its restfulness along with good service. Confident cooking, using fresh ingredients; a mixture of Italian and French dishes. Good value set meal. Excellent wine list. *LD (Reserve) open to 23.00. Closed Sun, L Sat.* A.Ax.B.Cb.Dc. **££.**

Lacy's 2 E 22
26 Whitfield St W1. 01-626 2323. A professional chef and his food-writing wife—Margaret Costa—combine to serve beautifully cooked food in this white-vaulted dining room. The atmosphere is relaxed, as is the service. Exceptional menu which changes seasonally: sorrel and cucumber soup, turbot en brioche with smoked salmon purée and fennel sauce, venison with cherries and chestnuts, medaillons of veal in cream and white wine sauce with mushrooms and stem ginger. Hot fruit salad or sorbet to follow. Good choice of wine. *LD (Reserve) open to 23.00. Closed Sun, L Sat.* A.Ax.B.Dc. **£££.**

Leith's 1 A 8
92 Kensington Park Rd W11. 01-229 4481. Tastefully offbeat decor in this converted Victorian private house complements the originality of Prue Leith's menu. Thoughtfully prepared and presented dishes from old 'Mrs Beeton' recipes as well as classical French cooking. Imaginitive selection of hors d'oeuvres, duckling, seafood in wine and cream sauce, spicy spring chicken, venison with black cherries. For dessert, try the ginger syllabub, orange and lemon soufflé. Cafetière coffee to follow or camomile or mint tea. Service is accomplished. Clarets and burgundies exceptional. *D (Reserve) open to 24.00. Sun to 23.15.* A.Ax.B.Dc. **£££.**

Marquis 2 G 17
121a Mount St W1. 01-499 1256. An opulently decorated room as befits its Mayfair setting and comfortable clientele. The basic menu offers a choice of French and Italian dishes, but perhaps more rewarding are the chef's suggestions, which change according to season and availability. Game is the winter speciality:

grouse, pheasant, wild duck and venison. The cooking is reliable, service engaging, and the wine list includes some very good bottles. *LD (Reserve) open to 23.00. Closed Sun.* A.Ax.B.Cb.Dc. **££.**

Meantime
47 Greenwich Church St SE10. 01-858 8705. Small, modern family concern, worth remembering on a trip to Greenwich. Short menu with a weekly speciality. Mussels, mackerel and gooseberry sauce, chicken and wine pancakes. *D (Reserve) open to 23.00. Closed Sun & Mon.* A. **£.**

Mirabelle   2 I 17
56 Curzon St W1. 01-499 4636. Justly famous Mayfair restaurant, renowned for the fine cooking and a magnificent wine cellar. Beautiful setting; the restaurant overlooks a garden; in summer the roof rolls back and meals are served under umbrellas. Vast menu; aiguillette de canetons aux truffes, homard Mirabelle, poulet à l'estragon. *LD (Reserve) open to 23.00. Closed Sun.* A.Ax.B.Cb.Dc. **£££.**

Neal Street Restaurant   3 I 23
26 Neal St WC2. 01-836 8368. Designed and owned by Terence Conran, this chic and modern restaurant is hung with Kasmin pictures and frequented by personalities from the contemporary arts world. Cooking matches the elegant decor; scrambled egg with smoked eel, king prawns wrapped in bacon, charcoaled on a skewer and served with a spicy mayonnaise, roast duck with apple sauce. Petit suisse with blackberry sauce to follow, or the excellent cheese board. *LD (Reserve) open to 23.00. Closed Sat & Sun.* A.Ax.B.Dc. **£££.**

Odin's   2 D 20
27 Devonshire St W1. 01-935 7296. Stylish brown and cream decor in this civilised, comfortable restaurant hung with paintings. Rich á la carte menu, frequently changed and inspired by various traditions of cooking. Mushroom pâté en brioche, stuffed roast duck, rack of lamb; also seasonal specialities such as game, lobster and mussels. Home-made ice-cream and lemon curd tart to follow. *LD (Reserve) open to 23.15. Closed Sun, L Sat.* **£££.**

Oslo Court
Prince Albert Rd NW8. 01-722 8795. On the ground
floor of a huge block of flats overlooking Regent's Park.
Its proprietor spent 12 years in the kitchens of the
White Tower and the skills he learned there are
apparent in the excellent cooking. The large
international menu embraces some good Balkan and
Central European dishes. Shashlik, duck Bosnaka,
escalope stuffed with cheese, fish soup. Sherry trifle or
fresh hot strawberries with home-made lemon ice-
cream for dessert. Garden for summer eating. *LD
(Reserve) open to 22.30. Closed Mon, Sun, L Sat.* **£££.**

Parkes   2 I 12
4 Beauchamp Place SW3. 01-589 1390. Staggeringly
original restaurant, with a garden downstairs, complete
with flowers and a fountain. The tables are a little close
together, but sample the fresh salmon en croûte and you
won't even notice the inconvenience. Also veal with
chestnut and cream sauce and Roquefort cheese with
Armagnac. *LD (Reserve) open to 23.00. Closed Sun, L
Sat.* A.Ax.B.Dc. **£££+.**

Peter's Bistro
65 Fairfax Rd NW6. 01-624 5804. A boon to anyone
hungry in NW6. Belongs to an ex-chef from the
Dorchester, who personally supervises the cooking.
Good roast beef, carré d'agneau and veal dishes.
Traditional four course set meal on Sun. *LD open to
23.30. Closed L Sat.* B.Dc. **££.**

Pollyanna's Bistro
2 Battersea Rise SW11. 01-228 0316. Useful for local
residents. On two floors—cool cream walls (pale yellow
downstairs), stripped floorboards, checked tablecloths
with candles and fresh flowers. Typical bistro fare—à
la carte with daily specialities. Attentive and relaxed
service. Summer barbecue. *D (Reserve) open to 24.00.
L (Reserve) Sun only.* A.Ax.B. **££.**

Pomegranates   5 Q 15
94 Grosvenor Rd SW1. 01-828 6560. Exudes the air of
a private dining room. Large tables, carefully selected
paintings, Tiffany lamps and an impressive
international menu. Welsh, Turkish, Malaysian, Greek,

French, Italian and Chinese dishes all prepared from first-class raw materials. Sample gravad lax with sweet mustard sauce, Welsh prawn pâté, or burek to start. Rognons de veau en brochette with romescu sauce, rond de gigot aux herbes de Provence and duck served with pomegranate and walnut sauce are some of the main courses. Sorbets, gâteaux and honey and cognac ice-cream to finish. Multi-national wine list. *LD (Reserve D) open to 23.15. Closed Sun, L Sat.* A.Ax.B.Dc. **£££.**

Red Onion Bistro   4 K 1
636 Fulham Rd SW6. 01-736 0920. Unpretentious, pleasantly basic and good value. French and English dishes with a sprinkling of Italian. Cannelloni, blinis, brochette of lamb, chicken Kiev, rolled breast of veal. *D (Reserve) open to 23.15. Closed Sun.* **£.**

The Ritz, Louis XVI Restaurant   2 I 18
Piccadilly W1. 01-493 8181. Pure Edwardian baroque with a fountain and a Boucher-like painted ceiling. A delightful change of époque to dine here gracefully and leisurely. Essential to dress correctly. Roast beef, oysters, mousseline of sole with champagne, fresh strawberries. Dance to a trio every night except Sun. *LD (Reserve L) open to 22.00.* A.Ax.B.Dc. **£££.**

Romano Santi   2 H 22
50 Greek St W1. 01-437 2350. Family concern established 1886. Spread over two floors, it still retains the charm of a Soho restaurant. Good value set lunches. Italian and Continental cooking. *LD open to 23.30.* A.Ax.B.Cb.Dc. **£.**

Royal Garden Hotel, Roof Restaurant   1 E 8
Kensington High St W8. 01-937 8000. The view over the tree-tops of Kensington Gardens has more appeal than the extravagant red decor. The menu is elaborate and sometimes overtaxes the kitchen. Fine wine list and painstaking service. With gipsy violins and a dance floor, this is a restaurant for an occasion. *D (Reserve) open to 01.30. Closed Sun.* B.Cb.Dc. **£££.**

Savoy Hotel Grill Room   6 K 23
Strand and Embankment WC2. 01-836 4343. World famous, well-deserved reputation for classic cooking and near-perfect service. Delightful panelled room, soft

lighting and a distinguished international menu with a very fine wine list. Attracts the elite from the artistic, literary and theatrical world. *LD (Reserve) open to 23.30. Sun to 22.30. Closed Sat.* A.Ax.B. **£££**.

September   4 L 4

457 Fulham Rd SW10. 01-352 0206. American designed restaurant, tables surround the circular garden. There is a separate bar and lounge with Liberty print walls. The menu is constantly changing depending on what is in season. Also offer a selection of vegetarian dishes. Avocado September, moussaka, salad of the month, quail, veal, calf's liver, carpetbag steak, nut roast. For dessert crème brûlée, cheesecake or choose from the sweet trolley. *D (Reserve) open to 24.00. Sun to 22.30.* A.Ax.B.Dc. **£££**.

Taste of Honey   1 A 8

2 Kensington Park Rd W11. 01-727 4146, 229 6731. Interesting semi-circular restaurant whose ambience is gradually moving up-market. French and English cuisine. Home-made soups, Stilton and fennel tart, escargots, to start. Wild duck in season. Jugged hare, venison ragoût, pigeon in port sauce, fresh crab, are among the specialities. Crème brûlée or meringue pie for dessert. *D open to 23.00. L Sat & Sun only. Closed Mon.* Ax. **££**.

William F's   4 K 7

140 Fulham Rd SW10. 01-373 5534. Informal, pine-clad bistro playing classical music for a predominantly young, arty clientele. The menu is thoughtful with some unusual dishes, prepared from good quality, fresh raw materials. It is frequently changed. *LD open to 23.30. Closed Sun.* **£**.

Italian

The following are but a short selection of by far the largest group of foreign restaurants in London. You can pick your way through the list and choose to eat cheaply or expensively. Several Italian restaurants, including pizza houses, are also mentioned in the 'Inexpensive eating' section. The food is of a consistently high standard.

Alcove   5 J 22
12 May's Court, St Martin's Lane WC2. 01-836 6140.
Tiny trattoria where you can enjoy a plate of excellent
home-made lasagne or a pizza and feel you have eaten
well. Useful before the theatre—often used by actors
and theatre staff. Speedy service. Meals available
throughout the afternoon. *LD open to 23.30. Closed
Sun, L Sat.* **££.**

Angelo's   2 I 19
42 Albermarle St W1. 01-499 1776. Popular trattoria
with very helpful and efficient service. Palatable food;
particularly crowded with shoppers at lunchtime. Fresh
grilled sardines, pâté, cold buffet and profiteroles to
follow. Choice of 'dish of the day'. *LD (Reserve L) open
to 23.30. Closed Sun, L Sat.* A.Ax.B.Dc. **££.**

Arlecchino   1 B 8
8 Hillgate St W8. 01-229 2027. A converted cottage
behind Notting Hill Gate Station. Small, popular with a
bistro atmosphere. Minestrone, veal chop in tomato
sauce, gruyère cheese and oregano, vegetables fresh
and well prepared. Background taped music. Italian
wine available by the glass. *LD (Reserve) open to 23.30.*
A.Ax.B.Dc. **££.**

Bertorelli Bros
19 Charlotte St W1. 01-636 4174   2 F 22
70 Queensway W2. 01-229 3160   1 A 11
Busy straightforward Italian eating places; good food
at reasonable prices from the family who make the
famous Bertorelli ice-creams. Standard Italian dishes.
LD open to 22.00. Closed Sun. **££.**

Biagi's   2 D 16
39 Upper Berkeley St W1. 01-723 0394. Small,
intimate trattoria decorated with fishing nets. Well-run
with a large, varied menu. Scaloppine alla crema,
entrecôte alla pizzaiola, tripe, saltimbocca. *LD
(Reserve) open to 23.00.* A.Ax.B.Cb.Dc. **££.**

Bianchi's   2 H 22
21a Frith St W1. 01-437 5194. Now over half a century
old. Still a simple family-run concern. Plain decor;
pleasant atmosphere; veal marsala, filetto Rossini,
chicken marescella and as good a plate of spaghetti

bolognese as you will find anywhere. *LD (Reserve) open to 23.00. Closed Sun.* A.Ax.B.Dc. **££.**

Borgo Santa Croce 4 M 8
112 Cheyne Walk SW10. 01-352 7534. A branch of San Frediano's. Spacious, friendly trattoria with an original menu. Fresh salmon pâté en croûte, crespoline florentina and venison steaks. *LD (Reserve) open to 23.15. Closed Sun.* A.Ax.B.Cb.Dc. **££.**

La Capannina 2 I 22
24 Romilly St W1. 01-437 2473. Typical, crowded Soho trattoria brightly decorated with familiar chianti bottles. Good home-cooked pasta with either plain cream or a variety of other sauces. Dishes of the day might include petto di pollo, vitello alla gianni; good selection of desserts. Music in the evening. *LD open to 23.30. Closed L Sat.* Ax.B.Dc. **££.**

Casa Cominetti
129 Rushey Green, Catford SE6. 01-697 2314. Local popularity gives this restaurant a certain interest. Reasonable Italian food in a gastronomic waste land. Home-made cannelloni, scaloppine oggi. *LD open to 21.00. Closed D Sun.* A.Ax.B.Dc. **££.**

Cecconi's 2 I 19
5a Burlington Gardens W1. 01-434 1500. Dine in elegant surroundings, amidst chic clientele. The pasta is home-made and especially recommended is their tagliatelli or ravioli or try a rare Italian delicacy carpacco. To follow home-made ice-cream. Service is attentive and helpful. *LD (Reserve) open to 22.45. Closed L Sat, Sun.* A.Ax. **£££.**

Chez Franco 1 A 10
3 Hereford Rd W2. 01-229 5079. Small neat restaurant with wooden chairs and benches, adorned with photographs of some of its more famous clients. Good menu of Italian and more international dishes—settina di Manzo, pizzaiola, fettucine al burro alla Romana. Very friendly service. *LD open to 23.30. Closed Sun, L Sat.* **££.**

Claudius 4 K 11
85 Sloane Ave SW3. 01-584 8608. Roman atmosphere given credence by columns, busts of the Emperor

Claudius, potted palms and window shutters. Beautifully moulded low ceiling. High standard Italian cuisine. Freshly made ravioli and cannelloni. Calamari, avocado with mozzarella and tomato, linguine served with plum sauce, duck, veal and fegato alla Veneziana. *LD (Reserve) open to 23.30.* A.Ax.B.Cb.Dc. **££.**

Colombina 5 J 20
4–5 Duke of York St SW1. 01-930 8279. Busy lunchtime restaurant. Simple decor, background music, and a wrought iron trellis hung with wine bottles divides the main room in two. Good spare ribs in hot sauce, gamberi funghi casa nostra, veal chop Arlecchino, veal alla Greca. Substantial sweet trolley. Mainly Italian wines. *LD (Reserve L) open to 23.00. Closed Sun.* A.Ax.B.Dc. **£.**

Como Lario 5 M 12
22 Holbein Place SW1. 01-730 2954. Lively and crowded trattoria. Very much the concern of the Italian family who run it—and who all work in it. Small menu. Cooking very sound. Swift service. Excellent pasta; gnocchi particularly noteworthy. Plenty of veal and chicken dishes, all reliable. Italian wines. *LD (Reserve D) open to 23.30. Closed Sun.* **£.**

Da Carlo
102 Kilburn Square, Kilburn High Rd NW6. 01-328 4930. Shopping precinct restaurant, but very much superior to its surroundings. Authentic Italian food served. Specialities include antipasto, frog's legs with garlic and tomato, raw mushrooms in cream. Vegetables included with each dish. Music. *LD (Reserve) open to 23.00. Closed Sun, L Sat.* A.Ax.B.Dc. **££.**

Don Luigi 5 L 12
33c King's Rd SW3. 01-730 3023. Good Italian food in a modern setting. Quarry tiles, high back chairs and modern paintings. Wide and varied menu with unusual specialities. Particularly good pasta and an excellent selection of hors d'oeuvres. *LD (Reserve) open to 23.30.* A.Ax.B.Cb.Dc. **££.**

Eleven Park Walk 4 L 6
11 Park Walk SW10. 01-352 3449. A place to be seen in if you want to attract the high fashion photographers

and designers. Smart clientele in a stylish cellar restaurant with Mediterranean ambience. Menu changed daily but home-made pastas are the speciality of the house. Also game, veal, fresh salmon trout, liver and tasty crudités with hot bagna cauda sauce. Select wine list. *LD (Reserve) open to 24.00. Closed Sun.* Ax. **££.**

Gatamelata   1 D 4
343 Kensington High St W8. 01-603 3613. Thronging with life, this popular Italian restaurant offers consistently reliable, authentic cuisine. Seafood salad, fresh mussels, mushrooms stuffed with venison pâté, quails, chicken pancakes, home-made tagliatelli, Italian sausage with beans. Big choice of desserts. Exclusively Italian wine list. *LD (Reserve) open to 23.30. Closed Sun, L Sat.* A.Ax.B.Dc. **££.**

Gennaro's   2 H 22
44 Dean St W1. 01-437 3950. Glamorous decor with busts of Roman heroes and antique cutlery. Wide choice of dishes: melon with Parma ham followed by chicken stuffed with mozzarella and ham, calves' liver and bacon cooked with herbs, stuffed quails. Also pasta specialities. *LD (Reserve) open to 23.00. Sun to 22.00.* A.Ax.B.Dc. **££.**

Gondoliere   1 F 8
3 Gloucester Rd SW7. 01-584 8062. Food served by waiters in white smocks and black ties amid murals of San Marco and other Venetian scenes. Welcoming, restful atmosphere. Cartoccio del gondoliere, sardines, fetuccine, Dover sole del gondoliere. *LD open to 23.30. Closed Sun, L Sat.* A.B. **££.**

Hostaria Romana   2 H 22
70 Dean St W1. 01-734 2869. Boisterous, busy, inexpensive restaurant. Consistently reliable Roman cooking. Regularly changed menu. Saltimbocca alla Romana, whitebait, agnellino al forno—zucchini or melitzane as vegetables. *LD (Reserve) open to 23.30.* A.Ax.B.Cb.Dc. **£.**

Luigi's   6 J 23
15 Tavistock St WC2. 01-240 1795. Crowded and very popular. Don't expect a table to yourself. It's Italian

bistro-style. Photographs of entertainment personalities on the wall. A marvellous place to eat before or after Covent Garden. The food is authentic and very good. Cannelloni, mussels grilled with breadcrumbs and garlic, veal and chicken dishes in good sauces. *LD (Reserve) open to 23.30. Closed Sun.* B.Dc. **££**.

Meridiana   **4 K** 7
169 Fulham Rd SW3. 01-589 8815. Comfortable, bright and spacious restaurant with an attractive white façade on the Fulham Road. Charming terrace for outside eating in summer. Piano music provides the background as you pick through a range of first-class Italian dishes. Magnificent display of hors d'oeuvres; also good tagliatelli, cotoletta Milanese and a wide choice of sweets. *LD (Reserve L) open to 23.30. Closed Sun.* A.Ax.B.Dc. **£££**.

Mimmo and Pasquale 5 M 16
64 Wilton Rd SW1. 01-828 6908. Pleasant restaurant
with fresh, white-washed walls and pink linen tablecloths. Covered terrace for summer eating. The
ingredients are all fresh, the cooking of a high standard.
Appetising starters, sea bass in white wine and pastas.
LD (Reserve) open to 23.30. Closed Sun, L Sat.
A.Ax.B.Dc. **££.**

Mimmo d'Ischia 5 M 16
61 Elizabeth St SW1. 01-730 5406. Bright, exciting
restaurant on two floors, decorated with autographed
photos of famous stars. Try the mixed seafood, the
scampi in brandy and cream sauce, fegato Carolina—
calves' liver with sage and butter, lamb with rosemary
or scallopine bella valeria—veal with mozzarella,
courgettes and tomato. Rich desserts. Speedy service.
LD (Reserve) open to 23.15. Closed Sun. A.Ax.B.Dc.
££.

Monte Bello 2 F 21
84 Great Titchfield St W1. 01-636 3772. Crowded
trattoria-style restaurant on two floors. Very popular at
lunchtime. Service is friendly and there is a happy
atmosphere which pervades the two rooms.
Uncomplicated, straightforward Italian dishes to
choose from: excellent pasta and pizza dishes. Or try
their pâté della casa for starters; fegato alla salvia,
picattine alla pizzaiola or pollo Monte Bello. All the
food is well prepared. *LD (Reserve L) open to 23.00.
Closed Sun.* **£.**

Montpeliano 2 I 12
13 Montpelier St SW7. 01-589 0032. Crowded
Knightsbridge restaurant. Fashionably decorated
mirrored rooms with plain white walls and lush green
plants. Basic Italian menu with frequently changing
regional specialities. Spaghetti dolcelatte, home-made
dumplings with herbs; veal Montpeliano—stuffed with
cheese, ham and garlic sauce; chicken parmesan—
breast of chicken cooked with aubergines and tomato
sauce. Try the chef's superb cold crêpes—his own
secret recipe—covered with ground biscuits and Tia
Maria. Regional Italian wines. *LD (Reserve) open to
24.00. Closed Sun.* **£££.**

Osteria Lariana   **2 H** 22
49 Frith St W1. 01-734 5183. Basic Italian fare without
great distinction, but a friendly, pleasant atmosphere.
Good pasta, fried calamari, veal in white wine. Tuscan
house wine. Taped music. *LD (Reserve) open to 23.30.*
Closed Sun. **£.**

I Paparazzi   **2 H** 22
52 Dean St W1. 01-437 3916. Bright, breezy,
welcoming restaurant. White walls, beige ceramic tiled
floor, fully air-conditioned and lots of plants.
Tantalising hors d'oeuvres counter near the entrance so
you can choose your own mixture. Many different
kinds of pastas in unusual shapes, with agnolotti as
something of a speciality. Good spaghetti alle vongole
with white sauce. Chicken dishes, osso buco and
octopus in a spicy tomato sauce. The owner Mr Alvaro
does his best not to compromise genuine Italian
cooking to suit the English palate and the results are
most enjoyable. *LD (Reserve L) open to 23.45.*
A.Ax.B.Dc. **££.**

Peter Mario   **2 I** 22
47 Gerrard St W1. 01-437 4170. Restaurant
established since 1933. Carefully cooked food in a
friendly setting. Seafood salad, tuna fish with onions
and beans, various pasta dishes or the speciality:
scaloppine Peter Mario—veal with almonds, raisins,
oranges in a sherry sauce, saltimbocca, beef stuffed
with mushroom and cheese, flavoured with basil.
Zabaglione, profiteroles or chestnut meringue to follow.
LD (Reserve) open to 23.15. Closed Sun.
A.Ax.B.Cb.Dc. **££.**

Pontevecchio   **1 I** 6
256 Old Brompton Rd SW5. 01-373 9082.
Comfortable, modern restaurant with tables outside
protected by box hedges. Tuscan cooking which
includes charcoal grilled lamb, calamari, pollo, and
uova girasole—a mixture of egg, liver and marsala.
Many varieties of pasta are also worth sampling. *LD*
(Reserve Sat & Sun) open to 23.45. A.Ax.B.Dc. **££.**

Rugantino   **2 I** 22
26 Romilly St W1. 01-437 5302. Friendly and reliable.
Tables packed together. Nut dishes are authentic and

very good. The chef takes a personal pride in his cooking. Fegato veneziano, frutti di mare, veal with orange and almonds. Some good vegetables: fennel and aubergines. *LD (Reserve L) open to 23.30. Closed Sun, L Sat.* A.Ax.B.Dc. **££.**

Sale e Pepe   2 I 13
13 Pavilion Rd SW3. 01-235 0098. Popular, noisy, fashionable restaurant belonging to an ex-manager of Mr Chow. Brisk lunchtime trade with Knightsbridge shoppers. Deep fried mozzarella with toast and anchovies, octopus salad, spaghetti carbonara, liver and special dishes of the day. *LD (Reserve) open to 23.30. Closed Sun.* Ax.B.Cb.Dc. **££.**

San Carlo
2 Highgate High St N6. 01-340 5823. Enterprising, lively and authentic. Somewhat noisy, particularly when the pianist is playing. Extremely good sliced aubergines in a spicy sauce, baby chicken with lemon and white wine, medaglioni San Domingo. Garden. *LD (Reserve) open to 23.00. Closed Mon.* A.Ax.B.Dc. **££.**

San Frediano   4 L 4
62 Fulham Rd SW3. 01-584 8375. Chaotic, busy trattoria. Exceedingly popular with a devoted following who don't mind the squashed tables and frenetic atmosphere. Beautifully laid out cold table, clam salad, snails, tagliatelli with cream and mushroom sauce. Good veal and liver dishes or crushed poussin cooked with brandy and herbs. Delicious zabaglione. *LD (Reserve) open to 23.30. Closed Sun.* A.Ax.B.Cb.Dc. **££.**

San Lorenzo Fuoriporta
Worple Rd Mews, Wimbledon SW19. 01-946 8463. Genuine whitewashed Italian establishment with welcoming exposed beams and portraits on the walls. Local following. Traditional menu. Some tables outside in summer. *LD open to 23.00.* A.Ax.B.Dc. **£££.**

San Martino   4 J 11
103 Walton St SW3. 01-589 1356. Lively, noisy restaurant with low ceilings, tiled walls and floors, decorated with Italian paintings. Aperitifs at the bar. Specialities include spaghetti San Martino—spaghetti cooked in a bag with prawns, mussels, scampi, squid,

white wine and garlic; or veal scarpano—cooked in vermouth and white wine with raisins and mushrooms. Fresh fruit salad or gâteaux for dessert. Good selection of regional Italian wines. *LD open to 23.30. Closed Sun.* A.Ax.B.Dc. **£.**

Sandro's   2 C 17
114 Crawford St W1. 01-935 5736. Comfortable even though a little cramped. Enjoy generous helpings of tasty osso buco, outstanding selection of meat and fish hors d'oeuvres, rack of lamb with Parmesan cheese and calves' liver prepared with sage and butter. *LD (Reserve L) open to 23.15. Closed Sun, L Sat.* A.Ax.B.Dc. **££.**

Santa Croce   4 M 8
112 Cheyne Walk SW10. 01-352 7534. Genuine Italian establishment. Various pastas, a good range of chicken and veal dishes; try mela stregata—a special Italian ice-cream in the shape of an apple and covered in chocolate. The waiter cracks the apple and pours in the strega. *LD open to 23.15. Closed Sun.* A.Ax.B.Cb.Dc. **££.**

La Terrazza   2 I 22
19 Romilly St W1. 01-734 2504. Beautifully designed white, elegant restaurant with spotlights and plants. Cramped but comfortable; stylish clientele. Good fettuccine and spaghetti carbonara. Scampi and Dover sole, pollo sorpresa—stuffed chicken breast with garlic butter, calves' brains with black butter, saltimbocca alla Romana, vitello tonnati—cold sliced veal with tuna and mayonnaise. *LD (Reserve) open to 23.15.* A.Ax.B.Cb.Dc. **££.**

Terrazza Est   6 J 26
125 Chancery Lane WC2. 01-242 2601. The old Mitre Inn transformed into an airy restaurant with Venetian ceiling and portraits on the wall. Many lawyers and journalists among the clientele. Good standard dishes. Exceptional sweet trolley. *LD (Reserve L) open to 23.30. Closed Sat & Sun.* A.Ax.B.Cb.Dc. **££.**

Tonino's   2 B 18
12 Glentworth St NW1. 01-935 4220. Friendly, slightly cramped restaurant. Some of the dishes are delicious; cooking usually reliable. Cozze marinara, pollo Tonino, veal in cream and mushroom sauce. Petits

fours are brought with coffee. A very happy place to dine, even without music. *LD (Reserve) open to 23.15. Closed Sun.* Ax.B.Dc. **££.**

Topo Gigio   2 I 21
3 Great Windmill St W1. 01-437 8516. Very appetising Italian food at reasonable prices. Good minestrone, cannelloni, petto di pollo, veal escalopes. The basement is particularly cosy. Helpful service. Conveniently off Piccadilly Circus, so best to book. *LD (Reserve) open to 23.30.* A.Ax.B.Dc. **££.**

Trattoo   1 E 6
2 Abingdon Rd W8. 01-937 4448. Good food under a glass roof, with ivy climbing trellises, and a giant mirror to give the illusion of space in a small room. Fresh raw materials and some fine cooking, though the sauces occasionally flag. Spaghetti vongole (with clams), fettuccine verdi alla cardinale, baby chicken cooked with rosemary. *LD (Reserve D) open to 23.00.* A.Ax.B.Cb.Dc. **£££.**

Vasco and Piero's Pavilion   2 G 21
Academy Cinema, Poland St W1. 01-437 8774. On the first floor of the Academy Cinema, with a separate entrance in Poland Street. Extremely good food. Worth a visit, even if you are not seeing a film. Seafood salad, fresh sea bass, stuffed aubergines, stinco arrosto. Gâteau soaked in Grand Marnier to follow. Guitarist evenings. *LD (Reserve L) open to 22.45. Closed Sun, L Sat.* A.Ax.B.Dc. **££.**

Japanese

Many of the Japanese restaurants in London have a private room decorated in the traditional manner, as well as a main eating area. You are expected to remove your shoes before entering and sit on tatami matting at a low table. Japanese eat all their dishes together as the various tastes, colours and textures are complementary.

Ajimura   3 I 23
51–53 Shelton St WC2. 01-240 0178. Agreeable, simple family restaurant. Various fish dishes;

vegetables are seasonal. The set dinner offers a good
selection of specialities particularly the sashimi (raw
fish in tasty soya sauce) and tempura (deep fried
seafoods or vegetables in a delicate piquant sauce).
Saké or plenty of green tea to accompany the meal. *LD
(Reserve) open to 23.00. Closed Sun, L Sat.*
A.Ax.B.Dc. **££.**

Aykoku-Kaku　　　　　　　　　　**6 N** 30
9 Walbrook EC4. 01-236 9020. Comfortable
restaurant popular with Japanese businessmen. Most
tastes and pockets are catered for, ranging from the
luxurious dining room where such specialities as
salmon in saké, sashimi and tempura are expertly and
delicately served, to the sushi bar with a selection of raw
fish on view. Good service from kimono dressed
waitresses. A variety of set lunches. *LD (Reserve) open
to 22.00. Closed Sat & Sun.* A.Ax.B.Dc. **£££+.**

Hokkai　　　　　　　　　　**2 I** 21
61 Brewer St W1. 01-734 5826. Traditionally dressed
waiters and waitresses will guide you through a long
and imaginative menu in this authentic, not over
expensive restaurant. Various set lunches include the
familiar choice of sashimi, tempura and teryaki-sauced
dishes. Set dinner includes king prawns and a rich fish
stew. Also à la carte selections. Try Japanese beer,
whisky or saké. *LD (Reserve) open to 22.30. Closed L
Sun, L Mon.* A.Ax.B.Dc. **££.**

Ikeda　　　　　　　　　　**2 G** 18
30 Brook St W1. 01-629 2730. Sushi chefs work at
great speed and in full view in this charming restaurant
with its own small courtyard. Set sashimi or tempura
meal. The à la carte menu includes some unusual
seasonal specialities. *LD (Reserve) open to 22.30.
Closed Sat & L Sun.* A.Ax.B.Dc. **£££.**

Masako　　　　　　　　　　**2 E** 18
6 St Christopher's Place W1. 01-935 1579. Authentic
Japanese restaurant with a number of private dining
rooms where you can eat sitting on the floor in true
Japanese style. The general restaurant is built around a
miniature Noh stage. Try the set sukiyaki or tempura
meals. Saké or Japanese beer to drink. *LD open to
22.30. Closed Sun.* Ax.B.Cb.Dc. **££.**

Mikado 2 D 18

110 George St W1. 01-935 8320. Close to the Japanese Trade Centre, this simple, restrained restaurant decorated with wood and tiles serves good, delicately prepared, familiar Japanese dishes. Sushi bar on street level, but downstairs for tempura, bean curd dishes, salmon, beef or chicken teryaki and other specialities. Occasional lapses in the service. Set meals available. *LD (Reserve) open to 22.30. Closed Sun, L Sat.* Ax.B.Dc. **£££.**

Saga 2 F 19

43 South Molton St W1. 01-408 2236. Traditional Japanese woodwork provides the decor in this small stark restaurant. The cooking is characteristic of the Japanese countryside, subtly flavoured. *LD open to 22.30. Closed Sun.* A.Ax.B.Cb.Dc. **£££.**

Suntory 5 J 19

72 St James's St SW1. 01-409 0201. Popular with ministers and officials from the Japanese Embassy. There are two main dining areas plus private rooms

which can be reserved for parties. Yakitori—pieces of chicken and vegetables served on bamboo skewers; usuzukun—thinly sliced raw fish served with a dip of sliced leeks, grated radish and lemon-flavoured soya sauce. Dobin-mushi—mixed meat and vegetables in clear fish soup seasoned with saké. Try fillet steak with shrimps as the main course. For dessert fruit mitsumame—fresh fruit salad with seaweed jelly. *LD (Reserve) open to 22.20. Closed Sun.* A.Ax.B.Cb.Dc. **£££+.**

Sushi Restaurant   **2 D 18**
61 Blandford St W1. 01-935 8311. In a street fashionable for Japanese restaurants. Usually one or two Japanese eating here. Sushi is the speciality. Choose from the raw seafood, pickles and other morsels laid out, and the sushi chef will prepare your choice. Also other dishes—such as sukiyaki or mizutaki. Seating is mostly at a counter. *LD open to 24.00. Closed Sun.* Dc. **££.**

Tokyo   **2 I 20**
7 Swallow St W1. 01-734 2269. Magnificent dining room, with traditionally laid tables and service; in the centre is a hollow tree. Try the sashimi—raw fish in season with soy sauce and spices, ohitashi—boiled green vegetables similarly sauced, miso soup—soyabeans with vegetables, seafood or bean curd. Various teryaki dishes, sukiyaki, or yose-nabe, chicken, prawns and a variety of fish combined with vegetables and traditional spices. Helpful service. *LD open to 23.00.* A.Ax.B.Dc. **££.**

Yamaju   **2 H 20**
16 Beak St W1. 01-437 2236. Eat in true Japanese style on tatami mats in private rooms. The interior of this unobtrusive but exquisite restaurant was built in Japan and reconstructed here by craftsmen. Even the chef, Mr Wematsu, one of the top cooks in Japan, was specially imported. There is no real menu but a selection of four set meals incorporating five, seven or nine special courses. Normally, the dishes required should be booked in advance and discussed with either the chef or the manager. Extra charm is provided by the kimonoed ladies who serve the meals. Booking is essential. *D (Reserve) open to 24.00.* A.Ax.B.Dc. **£££+.**

Jewish

The influence of German and Hungarian cuisine is strong. A Jewish menu might include latke (sweet, crisp fried potato pancakes), borscht (beetroot soup), pickled herrings as well as salt beef and chopped liver. In Britain many Jewish restaurants are no longer 'kosher'. A strict Jewish diet is governed by the laws of the Bible. Orthodox Jews are only permitted to eat the flesh of animals which have a cleft hoof and chew their cud, and fish which have scales. Do not be surprised if in a 'kosher' restaurant you cannot take milk in your coffee after eating a meal which includes meat. Dairy products should not be mixed with meat.

Bloom's
90 Whitechapel High St E1. 01-247 6001. Flourishing, bustling restaurant in the East End of London. Good wholesome portions of kreplach and kneidlach soup (dumplings), rich chopped liver and egg, renowned salt beef, gefilte fisch (sweet balls of chopped white fish either boiled or fried). To follow, try the lockshen pudding. Licensed or drink lemon tea with your meal. Also a branch at 130 Golders Green Rd NW11. 01-455 1338. *LD open to 21.30. Closed Fri 15.00, Sat, Jewish hols.* **£.**

Feld's   2 F 21
43 Mortimer St W1. 01-636 1045. In the garment district, north of Oxford St. Simple room, usually crowded at lunchtime. Excellent salt beef, chicken soup with barley, pickled herrings, chopped liver and lockshen pudding. Nearly everything, including the salt beef, is home-pickled. *LD open to 20.45. Fri to 15.30. Closed Sat.* **£.**

Goody's Original Kosher Restaurant   2 H 21
55 Berwick St W1. 01-437 6050. Sixty-year-old Jewish restaurant. Very comfortable and friendly. Good cooking and generous helpings of traditional fare. *LD open to 21.30.* A.Ax.B.Cb.Dc. **£.**

Grahame's Sea-Fare   2 H 21
38 Poland St W1. 01-437 3788. Kosher fish restaurant with a take-away service. Large and popular. Fish

served boiled, steamed or grilled with big portions of chips. Also pickled herrings and cucumbers. Good apfelstrudel or cheese blintzes. *LD open to 20.45. Closed Sun, D Mon.* **£.**

Harry Morgan's
31 St John's Wood High St NW8. 01-722 1869. All-Jewish menu care of Mrs Morgan. Simple and clean. Very reasonable prices. Gefilte fisch, latkes (sweet, fried, crisp potato pancakes). Hungarian goulash, black cherry cheesecake. *LD open to 22.00. Fri to 15.00. Closed Mon.* **£.**

Lebanese

A Lebanese menu nearly always features 'mezze' or hors d'oeuvres of some 20 dishes. Apart from charcoal grilled meats, cooking with spices such as coriander, garlic, cinnamon, nutmeg, cloves and ginger is much in evidence. Main courses with yoghurt are also very popular.

Al Amir 2 D 16
114 Edgware Rd W2. 01-262 6636. Uncomplicated decor with a gentle hint of the Middle East. Plenty of fresh flowers and courteous service. Large menu incorporating all the typical Lebanese dishes. Tabbouleh, houmous or motabal for hors d'oeuvres. Shawarma is a speciality worth savouring—slices of marinated veal grilled on upright skewers. Try also model—minced lamb with parsley, garlic and mint grilled and charcoaled on lettuce leaves. Lebanese wines. *LD (Reserve) open to 24.00.* A.Ax.B.Dc. **£££.**

Al Bustan 1 I 11
215 Brompton Rd SW3. 01-584 9388. Plain white interior with the odd potted plant characterises this restaurant catering for the increase of Arab visitors to London. To start with try the Kibby Nayeh—raw minced meat, crushed wheat, and spices or tabbouleh—again crushed wheat, parsley, mint, onions, tomatoes and lemon juice and to follow, the 'Special' to taste a variety of charcoal grilled meats. For dessert, the Katayef—a pancake stuffed with full cream

cheese. A cut above the familiar take-away kebab house—especially in price. Attentive service. *LD open to 23.45*. A.Ax.B.Cb.Dc. **££**.

Byblos **1 D 6**
262 Kensington High St W8. 01-603 4422. Lebanese cuisine with the familiar national dishes: tabbouleh, houmous, ful medannes. The wine list is limited, but try the Arak for a change. Lebanese recorded music and small portions for children. Also a take-away service. *LD (Reserve D) open to 24.00*. A.Ax.B.Dc. **££**.

The Lebanese Food Centre **5 K 12**
11 Sloane St SW1. 01-235 1896. This lively, friendly restaurant on two floors also has a shop selling Lebanese specialities. Try the fatayer—savoury pastries filled with spinach, onions and lemon, moujadora—lentil purée with onions and spices, tabbouleh, and to follow lamb or quail on a bed of spiced rice, pine kernels and almonds or marinated chicken pieces grilled on skewers. *LD (Reserve D) open to 23.30*. A.Ax.B.Dc. **££**.

Lebanese Restaurant **2 D 16**
60 Edgware Rd W2. 01-723 9130. Eat genuine Lebanese dishes in an oriental atmosphere. Mirrors, arches, dim wall lights and carved chairs in-laid with brass. Montabar—baked egg plant with sesame sauce, lemon, olive oil and garlic—or kibbeh—fresh raw lamb pourri served with spices and wheat. Various kebabs. Also meshwi, a selection of mixed meats cooked in onions. For dessert try katayef, an oriental pancake filled with cream cheese and nuts, or usmalieh, pieces of shredded wheat in cream and syrup. Arab music. *LD open to 24.00*. A.Ax.B.Cb.Dc. **££**.

Malaysian, Indonesian and Singapore

In all these countries, rice is the staple diet. To add variety and distinction, many spices are used and it is customary to add peanut sauce just before serving. The great Indonesian speciality is 'rijsttafel' or 'rice table'. It is basically rice, but with it come 20 or 30 small accompanying dishes. These include sambals, pickles, chutney and delicacies like ducks eggs, spiced fish fillets, deep fried meat balls, lamb vindaloo, spiced coconut. Another outstanding dish served in all these countries is 'satay', a kind of kebab. Bite-sized cubes of beef, veal or chicken, steeped in a special marinade containing coconut milk, are threaded onto skewers and grilled. They are then served with peanut sauce. Sweets and desserts are limited and it is best to choose fresh fruit. Malaysian and Singapore cuisine is in most respects similar to Indonesian. They are also extremely adept at preparing sea and fresh water fish. Non-alcoholic drinks are a speciality like 'Orchid Swizzle' and 'Angel's Delight' which may include pomegranate and tamarine juice, fresh coconut and sugar cane juice, mango and fresh ginger.

Bali
2 D 16

101 Edgware Rd W2. 01-723 3303/01-262 9100. South Sea island atmosphere with temple statues, bamboo furnishings, palms and bright murals. The waitresses wear batik print sarongs. Malaysian dishes on the ground floor; Indonesian banquet of 14 courses in the basement Bali room. Huge portions: giant king prawns with cucumber, chicken satay. Also good value set menus. *LD (Reserve) open to 23.30.* A.Ax.B.Cb.Dc. **££.**

Malaysian and Singapore
1 G 5

306 Earls Court Rd SW5. 01-370 2445. Clean and simple restaurant. Good Malaysian food attracting many oriental customers. Best to go with some friends to share a variety of dishes. Mee goreng (rice noodles with prawns and meat), kambing curry, sayor bayam (chopped spinach in a piquant sauce), bilai tandoori chicken. *LD open to 24.00.* Dc. **£.**

Mata Hari
3 C 25

38 Eversholt St NW1. 01-388 0131. Club atmosphere in a large, L-shaped room. Colourful Indonesian mural, purple and brown decor, dim lighting. Trio or pianist plays every night. Most people try saté, spicy chicken cubes or lamb on bamboo skewers, to begin. Enjoyable selection of specialities included in the set course meals

of the rijstaffel. Traditional Sumatran beef Rendang, sweet and sour fried prawns, gadu gadu salads, chicken in coconut. Sanbal is the spice which makes some of the dishes very hot. Good variety of fish. *LD (Reserve) open to 23.30. Fri & Sat to 24.00. Closed Mon.* A.Ax.Cb.Dc. **££.**

New Rasa Sayang   **2 I 22**
3 Leicester Place WC2. 01-437 4556. Hand-painted murals of Malaysian scenery help create a tropical atmosphere in this comfortable restaurant. An extensive menu of South-East Asian cooking with an emphasis on Malaysian specialities. Tasty satay, beef slices cooked in coconut, aubergines with dried fish in chilli sauce, spring rolls and some very good Indonesian salads. To finish, try ice kachang, a crushed ice pyramid made up of red beans, lychees, sweet corn, jellies, cream and syrup. *LD (Reserve) open to 23.15.* **£.**

Rasa Sayang   **2 H 22**
10 Frith St W1. 01-734 8720. Unpretentious restaurant serving authentic Singapore food. Try the chicken or beef with spicy peanut sauce, prawns or orange chicken. Satay, fish in tamarind sauce. *LD (Reserve D) open to 23.30.* **£.**

Mexican

Here can be found some of the world's most exciting cookery. Ground corn is the basic ingredient. The use of chilli in many dishes is also widespread. 'Tacos de pollo' are tortillas rolled into tubes and filled with shredded chicken and seasonings. 'Sopes' are dishes of corn dough fried and filled with cheese and chilli. Look out for specialities such as 'carne asada'—thin strips of beef fillet boiled and served with fried beans, hot green pepper and rich avocado sauce, and 'ceviche' marinated raw fish in lime juice, seasoned with oregano and chilli.

After Dark   **3 E 32**
145 Upper St N1. 01-226 4218. Brick walls, dark woodwork and an open fire. Tropical plants grow under a skylight and arches lead into the kitchen. Specialise in Tequila cocktails. For starters try ceviche—raw fish

marinated in lime juice; guacamole, crepas de camaron—served with chilli and cheese sauce. To follow enchiladas, mole poblano. For dessert flambé a almendra or ate de membrilla—quince preserve with cream cheese and crackers. Portions are very generous. *D (Reserve Thur, Fri & Sat) open to 24.00. Closed Sun.* Ax.Dc. **££.**

La Cucaracha   **2 H** 22
12–13 Greek St W1. 01-734 2253. London's first Mexican restaurant in the cellars of a converted monastery. Raw fish cocktail, arroz a la poblana, enchiladas. Spicy and delicious. Red beans, chillies and avocados are incorporated in many of the dishes. A guitarist entertains with Mexican tunes and songs in the evening. *LD open to 23.30. Closed Sun, L Sat.* A.Ax.B.Cb.Dc. **££.**

El Mexicano Taverna   **5 M** 12
62 Lower Sloane St SW3. 01-730 4637. Large, lively restaurant spread over two floors. Decor is that of a Mexican village cantina with wagon wheels on the wall and rough wooden tables. Downstairs for light music. Eat tacos, tamales, enchiladas, chillies and guacamole

around the fountain. Good mashed avocado pear, tomato and onion salads with coriander and hot chilli sauce. *D (Reserve) open to 24.00. Sun to 23.00.* A.Ax.B.Cb.Dc. **££.**

Open air eating

The Continental habit of eating out of doors can be very pleasant on a hot summer's day. Unfortunately very few London restaurants have managed to adapt to the variable weather. The following places have a few tables on the pavement or in the garden, in an enclosed courtyard or on a terrace. Some areas of London whip out tables and chairs at the first glimmer of sun, particularly the Greek restaurants around Charlotte Street and the cafés off Oxford Street.

Da Angela   4 K 9
119 Sydney St SW3. 01-352 2718. Very pretty Chelsea restaurant on two floors; pale decor with plenty of flowers and plants for a subdued atmosphere. Back courtyard for eating out in the summer. Italian regional dishes; all the pasta is home-made. Tomato and mozzarella salad, ham, salmon and prawns cooked with herbs, lamb and beans, veal veronelli. *LD (Reserve) open to 23.00. Closed Sun, L Sat.* A.Ax.B.Dc. **£.**

L'Artiste Assoiffé   1 A 8
122 Kensington Park Rd W11. 01-727 5111. Small shaded front garden. Informal and very worthwhile. A typical Kensington corner house close to the antique shops of the Portobello Road. Candlelight and the rather long intervals between courses create a leisurely atmosphere. Fairly authentic French food well cooked. Fondue bourguignonne, entrecôte au poivre, chicken stuffed with mushrooms in pastry, foie de veau des gourmets. *D open to 23.30. Sat L only. Closed Sun.* A.Ax.B.Cb.Dc. **££.**

Canonbury Tavern
21 Canonbury Place N1. 01-226 1881. Good place to take the kids, as there is a large garden at the rear with tables, chairs and swings. Food is served at the bar at

lunchtime; imaginative selection of cold salads, meats and pies with a few hot dishes. Also a proper restaurant offering fish, steaks, beef. *L open to 14.30. Closed Sat & Sun.* **£.**

Le Chef 2 D 15
41 Connaught St W2. 01-262 5945. Good French food in a cosy restaurant whose tables overflow onto the pavement in summer. Excellent fresh soups such as tomato or fish. Entrecôte au poivre, devilled kidneys. Good selection of sweets. *LD (Reserve) open to 23.30. Closed Sun & Mon, L Sat.* A. **£.**

La Famiglia 4 L 5
7 Langton St SW10. 01-351 0761. Warm, friendly Italian restaurant. White walls, ceramic tiled floor and a pretty rear garden which can seat about 32 people, in the summer months. An emphasis on southern Italian dishes. Many types of pasta, a renowned insalata casa nostra with mozzarella cheese, tomato and avocado pear. Sea bass in garlic and rosemary, grilled monk fish, calves' liver in sage and butter. Italian wines. *LD open to 23.30.* A.Ax.B.Dc. **££.**

Fingals 4 L 4
690 Fulham Rd SW6. 01-736 1195. Informal bistro-style restaurant that attracts a young clientele. The evening menu changes every month but may include seafood pie, chicken en croûte, duck. More informal fare at lunchtime. In winter, there is an open fire in the small pine-pannelled room and at the rear of the restaurant is a garden for summer eating. *LD open to 23.30. Closed Sun, L Sat.* B. **££.**

General Trading Company Café 5 K 12
144 Sloane St SW1. 01-630 0411. Popular refuge for women shoppers, offering morning coffee, lunch and afternoon tea. Small self-service ground floor room with outside terrace, more ample seating in the basement which leads on to a garden. Menu of about eight items changed two or three times a week. Fish and vegetable mousses, feuilleté de jambon, chicken and seafood salads, occasional pastas, osso buco, chicken florentine. Good selection of pastries, cakes and desserts. *L open to 16.45. Closed Sat & Sun.* **£.**

Il Girasole   **4 K 7**
126 Fulham Rd SW3. 01-370 6656. On the fashionable Fulham road; a few tables outside in summer. Cool and comfortable room inside if it's wet. Girasole is the Italian for sunflower; the restaurant plays upon this theme in its decor and a sunflower motif is even on the menu. *LD (Reserve) open to 23.30. Closed Mon.* Ax.B.Dc. *£.*

Holland Park Café   **1 C 5**
Ilchester Place W14. This is one of the better park cafés in London—perhaps because it is family-run. Situated in the centre of the Park, with tables outside in summer so you can enjoy the pleasing view. Apparently excellent coffee accounts for some famous regulars. They make their own soup but the food is generally cold, such as salads and quiches. Fresh cream gâteaux for desserts. *Unlicensed. LD open to dusk. Closed Dec & Jan. £.*

Jacaranda   **4 J 11**
Walton House, Walton St SW3. 01-589 0075. Delightful French restaurant in the former home of Lord Walton. The place also has connections with the Churchill family. Smart and polished ambience in a comfortable dining room that leads into a rear walled garden, which can seat about 50 people when the weather is fine. Specialities of the house are: coquille de fruits de mer, courgettes filled with prawns in a brandy and lobster sauce, veal Arlesienne, suprême de volaille Jacaranda, entrecôte au poivre and poussin cocotte grand-mère. Try the profiteroles for dessert. *LD (Reserve) open to 23.30. Closed Sun.* A.Ax.B.Dc. *££.*

Meridiana   **4 K 7**
169 Fulham Rd SW3. 01-589 8815. Comfortable, bright and spacious restaurant with an attractive white façade. Charming terrace for outside eating in summer. Piano music provides the background as you pick through a range of first-class Italian dishes. Magnificent display of hors d'oeuvres; also good tagliatelli, cotoletta Milanese and a wide choice of sweets. *LD (Reserve) open to 23.45. Closed Sun.* A.Ax.B.Dc. *££.*

Pontevecchio   **1 I 6**
256 Old Brompton Rd SW5. 01-373 9082. Comfortable, modern restaurant with tables out of

doors protected by box hedges. Brightly coloured awnings give good protection from the occasional shower. Tuscan cooking which includes charcoal grilled lamb, calamari, pollo, and uova girasole—a mixture of egg, liver and marsala. Many varieties of pasta are also worth sampling. *LD (Reserve Sat & Sun) open to 23.45.* A.Ax.B.Dc. **££.**

The Rose Garden   2 A 20
Queen Mary's Rose Garden, Regent's Park NW1. 01-935 5729. Open-air eating in a London park. Most unadventurous English food, but the surroundings at the right time of year make it absolutely idyllic. *LD open to 16.00 winter, 21.00 summer.* **£.**

Le Routier
Commercial Place, Chalk Farm Rd NW1. 01-485 0360. One of the better located restaurants in London. Situated by Camden Lock overlooking the canal, various craft workshops and the brightly painted barges. Seating outside in summer which creates a Mediterranean atmosphere. Food is fairly standard. Chicken Kiev, salads, stuffed trout, country pie, cold roast beef. Licensed. *LD (Reserve) open to 23.00. Closed Mon.* A.Ax. **££.**

San Lorenzo   2 I 12
22 Beauchamp Place SW3. 01-584 1074. One of London's best known Italian restaurants run by Lorenzo and his wife. Cool tiled entrance, modern prints on the wall; a bar and indoor garden (the roof rolls back in summer). Fashionable clientele who enjoy the excellent pasta and bollito misto served with an abundance of good sauces. Unusual veal and chicken dishes. Limited though reasonably priced wine list. *LD (Reserve) open to 23.30. Closed Sun.* **£££.**

Serpentine   2 F 12
Hyde Park W2. 01-723 8784. Overlooks the Serpentine. Food is fairly pedestrian but it is worth a visit if only for the excellent view of the park. Tables outside in summer. *LD open to 22.30.* A.Ax.B.Dc. **££.**

South of the Border   6 O 25
8 Joan St SE1. 01-928 6374. Charming spacious restaurant in a converted bed factory on the South Bank. Wood and brick walls hung with modern

paintings and embroidered rugs. Farmhouse atmosphere with a bar on the ground floor, overlooked by a balcony—outside terrace eating in summer. Frequently changed menu—avocado with crab, smoked haddock mousse, lamb cutlets with coriander and yoghurt, lamb kidneys in port and cream. Usually a vegetarian dish is available. To end the meal, ice-cream or cheese. *LD open to 23.30. Closed Sun, L Sat.* A.Ax.B.Dc. **££.**

Wild Thyme

96 Felsham Rd SW15. 01-789 3323. Pleasant French provincial cooking. Inventive menu, well-presented food. There is a glass-covered terrace on the pavement outside, whose doors open wide in summer. Menu changes regularly. *LD (Reserve) open to 23.00. Closed Sun & Mon.* A.B. **££.**

Out of town restaurants

The following are a small selection of good restaurants within an easy drive of central London. They are usually in or near historic towns or set in picturesque countryside.

Bell Inn

Aston Clinton, near Aylesbury, Bucks. Aylesbury 630252. Charming old inn, with a dining room facing on to the garden. Leather seating, gleaming glasses, an aroma of polished comfort. High quality, imaginative French food enjoyed by a strong local following. Game is a speciality. Superb wine list. *LD (Reserve) open to 21.30.* A.B. **£££.**

Boote House

Felsted, near Dunmow, Essex. Gt Dunmow 820279. Elizabethan house once lived in by the village 'boot-maker', now a cosy, informal family restaurant. The proprietor recites the small, French-based menu and you make your choice. It might include fish pâté, pork or meat balls in cream and mushroom sauce with pancakes to follow. *D (Reserve) open to 21.30. Closed Sun & Mon.* Ax.Dc. **£££.**

Christl's

118a High St, Berkhamsted, Herts. Berkhamsted 73707. An Austrian influence lends atmosphere to this plainly decorated restaurant unobtrusively situated above a parade of shops. Two rooms furnished with wooden tables and benches, a bar, candle-lit in the evenings. Food is interesting and always well cooked. Smoked haddock in a creamy spicy sauce; hot potted shrimps flavoured with nutmeg and mace; avocado with prawns in mustard, mayonnaise and leek sauce. Vienna schnitzel, excellent pepper steak, scampi and chicken Yassa, a West African dish. Fresh vegetables. Good coffee. *LD (Reserve Sat & Sun) open to 22.00. Fri & Sat to 22.30. Closed L Sat.* B. **£££.**

Cotsford Mill

Mill Lane, Hurst Green, Surrey. Oxted 3962. Beautiful setting for this restaurant which is part of a water mill. You can watch the water wheel working as you eat. Good boned duck, scampi, and steamed syrup sponge. Essential to book for a table with a view. Lovely on a summer evening. Bring your own wine. *D (Reserve) open to 20.30. Closed Sun & Mon.* **££.**

Duck Inn

Pett Bottom, Kent. Bridge 830354. Rustic 17th century inn, pleasantly tucked away from it all, run by a husband and wife partnership. Dining room with a blazing log fire and candle-lit tables. Small, original menu of mainly English dishes. Fresh shellfish stew, hare casserole, roast duckling with brandy and pineapple. Garden pears Cassis for dessert. Helpful service. Local Shepherd Neame bitter and a distinguished wine list. *LD (Reserve D) open to 21.15. Closed Mon, Tue.* Dc. **£££**.

Elizabeth

84 St Aldates, Oxford. Oxford 42230. Genuinely old restaurant of studied distinction. Linen table places, silver brass candlesticks, small panelled room. Interesting, frequently changed menu; skilful cooking. Smoked fish pâté, carré d'agneau, turbot, mussels fried in breadcrumbs, wild duck, entrecôte au poivre. Lemon syllabub to follow. Noteworthy claret and other wines. *D (Reserve). Sun L only. Open to 23.00.* A.Ax.B. **£££**.

Les Escargots

High St, Iver, Bucks. Iver 653778. Tiny, unpretentious Austrian-owned restaurant serving French specialities. Dishes are consistently well prepared: escalope de veau Oscar, oeufs en cocotte, filet de boeuf tartare. Limited choice of sweets. *LD open to 22.30. Closed Sun, L Sat.* A.Ax.B.Dc. **££**.

French Partridge

Horton, near Northampton, Northants. Northampton 870033. The 'French Partridge' is none other than Mr Partridge, the proprietor, who studied cooking in France. Victorian style, happy family air about the restaurant. Attentive service from local waitresses. Delicious four-course set dinner of French specialities that are frequently changed. *D (Reserve) open to 21.30. Closed Sun & Mon.* **££**.

Gravetype Manor Restaurant

East Grinstead, Sussex. Sharpsthorne 810567. Attractive Elizabethan manor house outside East Grinstead with fine gardens. Eat in the great dining room with its panels and open fire. Waiters in livery. Mostly French food. Huge helpings and rich ingredients. Salzburger Nockerln, morue fumée à la crème. Dover sole stuffed with prawns. Exceptional wine list including many imperial hocks and Gewurztraminers. *LD (Reserve) open to 21.00.* **£££+**.

Hintlesham Hall
Hintlesham, near Ipswich, Suffolk. Hintlesham 268.
The cookery writer and restaurateur Robert Carrier's
own mansion. Georgian façade in a park. David Hicks'
restoration of 18th century rooms within. Robert
Carrier is your host; you feel his guest at a banquet.
Unobtrusive butler-style service. Magnificent food at
inflationary prices. Brandade of smoked mackerel,
sliced sirloin sauce béarnaise, Roquefort quiche,
guinea-fowl with fresh limes, lamb au poivre vert. To
follow chocolate and chestnut bombe or famous Mrs
Moxon's lemon posset. *LD (Reserve) open to 22.00.*
Ax.Dc. **£££+.**

King's Lodge
Hunton Bridge, near Watford, King's Langley. King's
Langley 63506. A delightful old hunting lodge given to
Charles I in 1642. The interior is beamed and the lounge
covered in original Charles I crests. Smart, comfortable
dining room, velvet armchairs, plenty of light. Full
silver service. Extensive menu includes guinea fowl
chasseur, lobster thermidor, escargots, boned duck
cooked in port and orange sauce, sole, steak tartare and
entrecôte Diane. For dessert, flambés at the table are
the house speciality—crêpe Suzette, peach flambé,
cherries jubilee. *LD (Reserve) open to 22.30. Closed
Mon, D Sun.* A.Ax.B.Dc. **££.**

Lythe Hill Hotel, L'Auberge de France
Petworth Rd, Haslemere, Surrey. Haslemere 51251.
Manor house hotel set in the Surrey countryside with a
splendid view over gardens and a lake. One of the dining
rooms is 14th century. French 'international' cuisine.
Good, reliably prepared dishes. Efficient service. *LD
(Reserve) open to 22.15. Closed Mon, L Tue & January.*
A.Ax.B.Dc. **££.**

Milton Ernest Hall
Milton Ernest, Bedfordshire. Oakley 4111. In a
Victorian Gothic house by William Butterfield, now a
hotel. Everything is in period—pre-Raphaelite fabrics
and wallpaper. Lovely garden for a stroll. Proficient
cooking; English and French menu: prawns in garlic
mayonnaise, herring in mustard and oatmeal, pork in
cream sauce and charcoaled guinea-fowl. For dessert
try the lemon chiffon pudding or the fine Stilton. *LD
(Reserve) open to 21.30. Closed Mon, D Sun.* A.B. **£££.**

Moat House Hotel Restaurant

18 Southdown Rd, Harpenden, Herts. Harpenden 641111. Fine Georgian building which used to be a convent and was converted in the early 1970s. Formal restaurant, elaborately painted ceiling, chandeliers, draped curtains and alcoves. A la carte French cuisine menu. Polished service. Game, salmon and lobster in season. Dover sole Caprice, noisette de chevreuil aux cerises, carré d'agneau en croûte. To follow try omelette soufflé Grand Marnier. Some good vintage wines. *LD (Reserve) open to 21.00.* A.Ax.B.Cb.Dc. **£££.**

Old Crown Inn

Messing, Essex. Maldon 815575. Informal, thriving pub with a welcoming atmosphere. The proprietor and his partner do the cooking. Menu changes quarterly. Extremely good oeufs Argenteuil, snails with ham and almond sauce, quails stuffed with pâté; rich gâteaux, orange fool. No children under 14 in the dining room. *LD (Reserve D) open to 21.30. Closed Sun, D Mon, L Sat.* **££.**

O'Rorkes

Pound Hill, Alresford, Hants. Alresford 2293. Bright green and pink decor with candle-lit tables provide a welcome haven for harassed travellers. Harpsichordist entertains on Weds. Excellent food and wine. Crespolini, lobster thermidor, pike quenelles, roast veal and raisins; chocolate mousse with liqueur to follow. *LD (Reserve) open to 21.30. Closed Sun.* A.B. **££.**

Pastori's Farmhouse Restaurant

Selsdon Park Rd, Addington, Surrey. 01-657 2576. Modest, intimate and personal. The proprietor takes trouble to greet visitors and advise them on the menu, as they sip a glass of sherry propping up the bar. Very good French cooking with Italian undertones prepared by an Irish chef. Soups are home-made, vegetables are fresh, and the veal dishes are as good as you will find anywhere. *LD (Reserve) open to 22.00. Closed Sun & Mon.* A.Ax.B.Dc. **£££.**

The Refectory

6 Church Walk, Richmond, Surrey. 01-940 6264. A small restaurant set in the precincts of Richmond parish church. Good, wholesome English cooking that

concentrates more on pies and casseroles than roasts. Fresh vegetables daily and home-made soups. Pews constitute, most suitably, part of the seating arrangements. *LD (Reserve) open to 20.45. Closed Mon, D Sun to Wed.* **££.**

Sopwell House Hotel
Cotton Mill Lane, St Albans, Herts. St Albans 64477. Within easy reach of London, a grand Georgian house set in two-and-a-half acres of land. The elegant dining room overlooks a delightful garden and weather permitting, there is outside eating in the summer. A predominantly French menu prepared from good fresh ingredients by French chefs. Flambé cooking at the table is the house speciality. Scampi Martini, filet mignon, lobster thermidor, steak tartare, coquille St Jacques, turbot rosslyn, sea bass in season and rainbow trout in lemon and capers. For hors d'oeuvres try deep fried pancakes with chicken, peppers and mushrooms, or Stilton pâté. Comprehensive wine list. *LD (Reserve) open to 21.00.* A.Ax.B.Dc. **£££.**

Sundial
Herstmonceux, near Hailsham, Sussex. Herstmonceux 2217. A pretty 16th century cottage in the Sussex Downs, where an enterprising couple cook very good Italian and French dishes. Fish, including lobsters, comes from Dieppe. All raw materials are of the best according to the season. Stuffed courgettes, rouget au romarin, followed by peaches in brandy and apple flan. Outstanding set lunch. Fine clarets. *LD (Reserve) open to 22.00. Closed D Sun, Mon, January and last two weeks in August.* B.Dc. **££.**

Le Talbooth
Gun Hill, Dedham, Essex. Colchester 323150. A mile from Dedham, in Constable country. Delightful timbered inn on the banks of the Stour. A series of dining rooms. Ambitious, mainly French cooking. Also local specialities like Colchester oysters and home-cured Suffolk ham. Particularly good selection of sweets, including kirsch meringue gâteau and brandy snaps. *LD (Reserve) open to 21.00.* A. **£££.**

Toastmaster's Inn
Church St, Burham, Kent. Medway 61299. Amazing

collection of over 600 wines, having won an award for the finest collection in the British Isles. The menu leans towards the nouvelle cuisine and changes fortnightly, but may include crab mousse, filet de porc en croûte, blackcurrant fool. *LD (Reserve) open to 22.00. Closed Sun & Mon.* B. **£££**.

Trout Inn

St John's Bridge, Lechlade, Glos. Lechlade 52313. Seven-hundred-year-old inn on the edge of the Thames. Stone floor, exposed beams in the small dining room decorated with carriage lamps and candle-lit in the evening. Fresh trout, prepared in various ways, is the speciality. Also other English dishes like braised gammon and roast duck with orange. *LD (Reserve) open to 21.30. Closed Mon.* A.B. **££**.

Waterside Inn

Ferry Rd, Bray-on-Thames, Berks. Maidenhead 20691. One of the most beautiful settings for some of the best French food outside London. The dining room french windows look out on to the water and the willows. Faultless cuisine. Pâté de poisson à la Guillaume Tell, soufflé de homard, chicken with truffles followed by tarte au citron. Some fine French wines. *LD (Reserve) open to 22.00. Closed Mon, D Sun.* A.Ax.B.Dc. **£££+**.

White Hart Hotel Restaurant

Thames St, Sonning-on-Thames, near Reading, Berks. Reading 692277. Glorious riverside setting. A famous rose garden sloping down to private secluded moorings. Medieval banquets held in the Elizabethan restaurant. Haute cuisine in the elegant Regency room with red velvet and gold decor. Adjoining cocktail bar. Wide range of hors d'oeuvres from the trolley, jambon d'Ardennes et melon, oeufs Florentine, home-made soups. In addition to the à la carte, there is also a carte des gourmets including such dishes as truite de rivière Georges Sand, l'angoustine a la Veneziana (cooked at the table) and médaillons de boeuf bourguignonne. Own pâtisserie. Carefully selected wines. *LD (Reserve) open to 21.30.* A.Ax.B.Cb.Dc. **££**.

Wife of Bath

4 Upper Bridge St, Wye, Kent. Wye 812540. Excellent, unpretentious terraced house; civilised and

comfortable. Imaginative cooking based on top-class ingredients. Tartlet of red mullet, ham and leeks in Cumberland sauce, baked sea bass, lobster en croûte, elderflower sorbet. *LD (Reserve) open to 22.00. Closed Sun & Mon.* **££.**

Polynesian

Beachcomber 2 I 18
Mayfair Hotel, Berkeley St W1. 01-629 7777. Dinner dancing in South Sea Hawaiian setting. Alligators complete the tropical atmosphere. Try the exotic drinks and sample chicken momi and steak luau. *D open to 02.00. Closed Sun.* A.Ax.B.Dc. **£££.**

Trader Vic's 2 I 16
Hilton Hotel, Park Lane W1. 01-493 8000. Atmosphere of Pacific Islands and the orient in both decor and food. Dimly-lit with shells and shark's teeth on the walls and taped Hawaiian music. Begin with a fresh, exotic cocktail which might appear with floating lilies. Fried prawns, crab in mustard sauce, Tahitian fish soup. The Indonesian marinated lamb roast has a delicious subtle flavour and is served with a peanut

sauce. To follow, pancakes, unusual ice-creams or a variety of coffees. *LD open to 24.00. Closed L Sat.* A.Ax.B.Cb.Dc. **£££+.**

Pub restaurants

The mysteries of the licensing laws need not worry you when reading this section. The pubs have been chosen either for their excellent food (good traditional English cooking or French classic), or for their famous historical background. Often, for both. Most of the pubs mentioned also have a cold buffet service in the bar. The restaurant area is usually set aside. *Also see 'Riverside eating.'*

Admiral Codrington   **4 J** 11
17 Mossop St SW3. 01-589 4603. Good Chelsea 'local'. Gaslit, Victorian interior with a large selection of toby jugs. Varied menu: escargots, game pie, hot curries. Also salads and quiches. *LD open to 22.45.* A.Ax.Dc. **£.**

Blue Posts   **2 I** 19
6 Bennet St SW1. 01-493 3350. Upstairs restaurant in a plush area behind the Ritz Hotel. Wood-pannelled room with an intimate atmosphere. English carvery offering a choice of beef, turkey, pork or lamb. Waiter or self-service. Also a large cold table and pre-theatre meals available. Downstairs, a decent snack bar in a genteel, traditional pub. *LD (Reserve L) open to 22.00. Closed Sat & Sun.* A.B.Cb.Dc. **££.**

The Bull's Head
Lonsdale Rd SW13. 01-876 0185. One of the foremost jazz pubs in the country, attracting big name players from Britain and the USA. In converted stables, behind the pub, is a restaurant called the 'Head and Tail'. Inside the old stalls and troughs are preserved. Good English menu including trout, rack of lamb, home-made steak and kidney pie, spare ribs, steaks, sherry trifle, syllabub, flans and banana and walnut cream whips. Traditional Sunday lunch. *D (Reserve) open to 23.00. Sunday to 15.00.* **££.**

Cherry Tree

The Green, Southgate N14. 01-886 0248. Old coach house, with original wooden-beamed whitewashed interior. English and French cooking, with varying specialities every week. Generous steaks, charcoal-grilled; also scampi. One of the best pubs in North London with plenty of atmosphere and a core of regulars. *LD open to 22.15. Closed D Sun.* A.Ax.B.Dc. **££.**

Cheshire Cheese (Ye Olde)   **6 K 26**

145 Fleet St EC4. 01-353 6170. With medieval cellars, built-over after the Fire of London, this pub's name is no mere gimmick. Low-ceiling'd interiors, oak tables, sawdust on the floor and probably much like it was when Dr Johnson used to drop in. Sound English cooking includes best roast beef, steak and kidney pie and pudding and traditional sweets like bread and butter pudding. *LD (Reserve) open to 20.30. Closed Sat & Sun.* **££.**

Cock & Lion   **2 E 19**

62 Wigmore St W1. 01-935 8727. Cheerful and full with a pleasant first-floor restaurant with wood-panelled walls. Traditional English cooking with a limited range of starters and sweets, but very fine grills and steaks; you can watch the grilling while you wait. *LD open to 22.15. Closed Sun, L Sat.* A.Ax.B.Dc. **££.**

Cock Tavern (Ye Olde)   **6 K 26**

22 Fleet St EC4. 01-353 8570. Small but good journalists' tavern with literary and Dickensian associations and mementos. One large dining room usually packed full with local office workers and journalists. English carvery, lemon sole, trout with capers, puddings and pies; try the special steak, kidney and mushroom pie. Breakfast daily. *L open to 14.30. Closed Sat & Sun.* A.Ax.B.Dc. **££.**

Dirty Dick's   **6 N 33**

202–4 Bishopsgate EC2. 01-283 5888. The original pub to be named after Nat Bentley, well-known 18th century miser and Dirty Old Man 'If I wash my hands today, they will be dirty again tomorrow...' This pub's extensive vaults, with mummified cats, are kept artificially dirty. Hot and cold snacks, steaks, grilled chops, curry. Smoked herring for starters and apple pie or cheeseboard to end the meal. Decorated with stickers and pieces of paper signed by visitors from all over the world. *LD open to 20.00.* A.x.B. **£.**

French Revolution
180 Lower Richmond Rd SW15. 01-788 0925. Recent conversion of the stable area at the back into a bistro has retained the horse brasses and other former stable adornments. Menu is chalked up on a blackboard in true bistro style, with regular changes and specialities of the day. The wine list is also on the board and there are some good bin ends. *LD open to 21.45. Closed Sun, L Sat, D Mon.* A.Ax.B.Dc. **££.**

George Inn   6 Q 27
77 Borough High St SE1. 01-407 2056. Galleried 17th century coaching inn, once patronised by Dickens and mentioned in 'Little Dorrit'. Traditional draught beer served. Choice English table d'hôte, à la carte as well with steak, chops and fish. Refectory style long tables are most appropriate in this setting and in summer the large courtyard is used as an open air theatre. *LD open to 21.00. Closed Sun.* A.Ax.B.Dc. **£.**

George & Vulture   6 N 30
3 Castle Court EC3. 01-626 9710. This 14th century inn maintains its historical atmosphere and emphasises its connection with Dickens—it is mentioned in 'The Pickwick Papers'. Silver tankards for downing one's pint, and a traditional English menu with generous steaks, daily change of roasts, and fine puddings and pies. *L open to 15.00. Closed Sat & Sun.* A.Ax.B.Dc. **££.**

Grenadier   2 I 14
18 Wilton Row SW1. 01-235 3074. Mews pub with its ceiling covered with wine labels. Duke of Wellington played cards here. The back half has prints of guardsmen and weapons on the walls. Good English restaurant, specialities of Norfolk duckling, steak and kidney pie, pineapple Grenadier. *LD open to 21.30.* A.Ax.B.Dc. **££.**

The Grove Tavern   2 I 12
43 Beauchamp Place, SW3. 01-589 5897. A tavern since the late nineteenth century and now handy for

Knightsbridge shoppers. Restaurant upstairs with unusual solid slate topped tables. Traditional English fare—steak and kidney pie, braised liver, casseroles, fish and chips. All the ingredients are fresh and the food home-made. *L open to 14.40.* A.B.**£.**

Horseless Carriage

Hatch Lane, Chingford E4. 01-529 1020. Everything here for nostalgic travellers on the Brighton Belle. The old train is displayed in the front window and provides the theme throughout the pub. Basic English cooking with generous steaks and Dover sole. Large drinking patio outside. *LD open to 22.00. Closed L Sat.* **£.**

Island Queen   3 F 32

87 Noel Rd, N1. 01-226 0307. Popular Islington meeting place. Three larger-than-life Victorian models in lace-up underwear and black stockings are suspended over the bar. Beautiful leaded mirrors adorn the walls. The restaurant is no less attractive with Kentia palms, elaborate paper flower arrangements and many local artists' prints. English and French cuisine, very generous helpings. Grilled tandoori prawns, Rocquefort mousse, deep fried mushrooms with cucumber and garlic mayonnaise, home-made soups. Fresh fish from the market, beef in mustard and cream sauce. Notable vegetables, but a small selection of desserts. Special menus can be ordered for parties and business lunches. Hot food at the bar as well. *D (Reserve) open to 22.45. Closed D Sun, D Mon.* **££.**

Jack Straw's Castle

North End Way NW3. 01-435 8885. Recently redecorated, modern and comfortable with an extensive view high over the Heath. Well worth booking in advance to make sure of a window seat. English cooking with a Continental touch. Dover Sole, steak au poivre, fresh roasts from the trolley daily. *LD (Reserve) open to 21.45. Closed D Sun.* **££.**

King's Head   3 E 32

115 Upper St N1. 01-226 1916. Probably the best known and most widely reviewed of the theatre pubs. Decorated with theatre handbills. Restaurant is part of the bar and theatre at the back. Set menu includes charcoal grills, spare ribs, stew or curry. Baked apple

pudding. Lunchtime and evening performances. *LD (Reserve) open to 20.00. Closed Sun.* **£.**

The Orange Tree
45 Kew Rd, Richmond, Surrey. 01-940 0944. The cellar restaurant is traditionally comfortable, with old panelling, brick walls and Spanish wrought-iron fittings to create a relaxing atmosphere. Plays performed by the Richmond Fringe Theatre Group. European food, cooked with flair and appetisingly presented: osso buco, braised rabbit, pork in fennel, lasagne, paella, ham on the bone, curries. Very good value. *LD open to 21.45. Closed Sun.* **£.**

Penny Black   6 L 31
Tentor House, Moorfields, Moorgate EC2. 01-628 3675. As the name indicates, the pub is covered with an enormous number of original stamps, as well as many philatelic prints taken from the GPO's collection. The dining room is separated from the drinking area although not closed off. Basic English fare includes gammon, steaks, seafood platter and plat du jour. *L open to 14.30.* A.B. **£.**

Pindar of Wakefield   3 G 27
328 Grays Inn Rd WC1. 01-837 7269. *The* pub to go for old time 'music hall'—but pick your evening or you may find ragtime or modern jazz playing instead. Decorated with music hall mirrors and posters, with loads of cheerful participating regulars. Limited menu but reliable: scampi in a basket, roast chicken. Dinner served on music hall nights. *D open to 21.30.* **£.**

Prince Regent   **2 D** 19
71 Marylebone High St W1. 01-935 2018. Attention to
detail in the Regency fittings and a unique collection of
cheese dishes. French and English cooking; especially
good steaks, grills and lamb cutlets. Eat in the smaller
room or in a larger area where you can watch the
cooking. *LD open to 22.00. Closed Sun, D Sat.*
A.Ax.B.Dc. **£**.

Prospect of Whitby
57 Wapping Wall E1. 01-481 1095. Six hundred years
old. Famous Pepys tavern in dockland with terrace
overlooking the Thames. Nautical souvenirs, old curios
and fine pewter. Excellent inventive French cuisine,
with many house specialities: crêpes Prospect of
Whitby—seafood-stuffed pancakes, wine sauce on
rice; or mushroom Prospect—with pâté and cream.
Also veal cordon bleu; wide selection of grills. Book
early. *LD (Reserve) open to 21.45. Closed, D Sun, D
Mon.* A.Ax.B.Dc. **££**.

The Queens
49 Regents Park Rd NW1. 01-722 6006. Pleasant
Edwardian interior. Named after the Queens Victoria
and Alexandra. English grills with special roasts of the
day, steak and kidney pie and game casserole. Try their
home-made apple pie if you've still got room. *LD open
to 22.00. Closed Sun, L Sat.* B.Dc. **£**.

Red Lion   **6 M** 29
17 Watling St EC4. 01-248 2785. Modern building,
comfortable, pleasant pub with a very fine wine list,
especially clarets. Good restaurant, with an extensive
menu, and many worthy specialities. Entrecôte
chasseur, fresh lobster, fillet steak forrestière, game in
season, salmon. Follow this with mangos, strawberries,
or imperial banana split. The list of hors d'oeuvres is
impressive. *L open to 15.00. Closed Sat & Sun.* A.B.
££.

Red Lion   **2 H** 17
Waverton St W1. 01-499 1307. A 17th century
Mayfair inn with forecourt. Inside Royal Academy
prints and paintings hang in comfortable surroundings.
Traditional English food, with best Scottish beef for the
steaks and grills. Melon and avocado starters and a

good cheeseboard or a really fresh fruit salad to end the meal. *LD (Reserve) open to 21.45. Closed Sun.* A.Ax.B.Dc. **£££.**

The Rising Sun   3 B 33
55 Brooksby St N1. 01-606 2844. Enthusiastically restored Victorian pub with a small rear garden. Original eighteenth century prints of London line the walls, genuine Britannia tables and comfortable seating. The former living accommodation upstairs has been converted into a good value restaurant. An Italian chef prepares steaks, roasts, pork chops in a spicy sauce, fish and home-made apple pie. A friendly atmosphere attracting local business people and young professionals who wish to avoid the area's more expensive restaurants or the ethnic joints. *LD (Reserve) open to 21.30. Closed L Sat, D Sun, D Mon.* **£.**

Roebuck
130 Richmond Hill, Richmond, Surrey. 01-940 0607. A magnificent view of the Thames valley. Three dining rooms, candle-lit in the evenings, with hunting scenes on the walls. Quality cooking of grills and traditional dishes. Prawns and mushrooms, duck with peaches and brandy, salmon steak. To follow rhum baba or Florida cocktail. *D (Reserve) open to 21.45. Closed D Sun.* **££.**

Rossetti
23 Queen's Grove NW8. 01-722 7141. Modern, attractive St John's Wood pub-trattoria. Light and airy with Rossetti etchings on the walls and plenty of green plants. Authentic Italian menu: osso buco, all sorts of veal, and regular changes of house specialities. Wide variety of sweets. A large menu catered for by two Italian chefs. Varied price range. *LD (Reserve) open to 23.30.* A.Ax.B.Dc. **££.**

St Stephen's Tavern   5 M 21
10 Bridge St SW1. 01-930 2541. Victorian tavern named after the tower of Big Ben. Good views from the bar, which is lined with old engraved mirrors. Upstairs in the restaurant a bell connects the House of Commons to the Members for 'Divisions'. Traditional English menu, wide range of hors d'oeuvres; best Scotch roast beef, steak, kidney and mushroom pie or pudding. Sherry trifle to follow. Original coloured

cartoons of bygone MPs gaze down on their successors. *LD (Reserve L) open to 21.00. Closed D Sun.* A.Ax.B.Dc. **££**.

Sherlock Holmes 5 K 22

10 Northumberland St WC2. 01-930 2644. Extensive collection of relics of the famous fictional detective. The inside is a replica of Holmes' study at 221b Baker St. English and French cooking are elegantly matched: try the chicken, called 'the Sherlock Holmes', also grills, scampi, sole, trout. This pub, formerly the 'Northumberland Arms' is mentioned in the 'Hound of the Baskervilles'. *LD open to 21.15. Closed Sun, L Sat.* A.Ax.B.Dc. **££**.

Spotted Dog

212 Upton Lane E7. 01-472 1794. Handsome 17th century inn isued by the city merchants during the Great Plague. Dick Turpin connections, though the interior decor concentrates on the earlier Tudor theme. Oak beams, plaster whitewash, prints. A typical sound grill menu, rump, sirloin or fillet steak, or plaice. Very full of present day City merchants at lunchtime. *LD open to 22.00. Closed L Sat.* A.Ax.B.Dc. **£**.

Tattersall's Tavern 2 H 13

Knightsbridge Green SW1. 01-584 7122. Built on the former site of Tattersall's offices, this pub preserves the memory of their long association with the horse world. The restaurant has pictures of famous horses and race-meetings, and the bar has memorials of Tattersall Yard at the Hyde Park period—look at the replica of the original pump, which is now in the paddocks at Newmarket. The comfortable restaurant also has oak panelling and serves quality cooked food from a wide menu. Try Tattersall's mixed grill, kidney Turbigo, veal escalopes, or Virginia honey roast ham from their cold buffet. *L open to 14.30. Closed Sat & Sun.* A.Ax.B.Dc. **££**.

Riverside eating

The following restaurants, many of them historic inns, are either on the river or a few minutes' walk from it. They all offer good food. Often fishing or boating can be arranged if you have planned a day out. But there is nearly always plenty to watch, and usually a towpath to walk along. All the restaurants are within 60 miles of London.

Anchor   6 O 28
Bankside SE1. 01-407 1577. The original pub was only 200 yards away from the Globe theatre but was destroyed by the fire of 1666. The present building is 18th century. Three dining rooms, one with a minstrel's gallery. Exposed beams, large open fireplaces and plenty of antique odds and ends to look at while eating, including the first edition of Dr Johnson's Dictionary. English menu: smoked trout, Dover sole, chicken chasseur and a wide range of grills. Fresh fruit salad or elaborate gâteaux to follow. *LD (Reserve) open to 22.00. Closed Sun.* A.Ax.B.Cb.Dc. **££.**

Angel
101 Bermondsey Wall, East Bermondsey SE16. 01-237 3608. A 16th century Thames-side tavern built on pillars, with extensive view of the river and the Pool of London. Low ceilings, wooden beams, walls hung with prints of the area as it used to be. Continental cuisine: moussaka, salmon koulibiak, steak chasseur, chicken Kiev, scampi provençale. Extensive cheeseboard. *LD open to 21.45. Closed Sun, L Sat.* A.Ax.B.Dc. **££.**

The Captain's Cabin   6 R 32
St Katherine Yacht Haven, East Smithfield E1. 01-480 5907. You might well think this was the Mediterranean with the fine views over the yacht harbour. The restaurant is on two floors in a converted police-station and decorated to give an old world atmosphere. Rather basic English food—steaks, casseroles, sole and home-made steak and kidney pie. *LD (Reserve) open to 23.00.* A.Ax.B.Dc. **££.**

Compleat Angler, Valaisan Restaurant

Marlow Bridge, Bucks. Marlow 4444. A magnificent setting in an old and historic hotel. The whole restaurant looks on to the river. Wooden-beamed ceiling, highly polished tables, river scenes on the walls and comfortable green leather-backed chairs. Enjoyable French cuisine with paupiettes de saumon fumé or fresh pear stuffed with Stilton to start. Filet de boeuf Wellington on request. Excellent fish, carré d'agneau aux herbes de Provence and roast duck with curacao and orange sauce. Twice a week there is a pianist in the evenings to add an extra touch of class to the romantic atmosphere. *LD (Reserve) open to 21.30.* A.Ax.B.Cb.Dc. **££.**

Contented Sole

80 High St, Burnham on Crouch, Essex. Maldon 782139. Popular sailing village. Not on the river but very close. Good local fish is the speciality. Capable cooking. Friendly atmosphere. Dinghy racing to watch in the summer months at weekends. *LD open to 21.30. Closed Sun & Mon.* **££.**

Cutty Sark

Ballast Quay, Lassell St SE10. 01-858 3146. Quiet Georgian pub with wooden interior. Overlooks the river and wharves, near the famous *Cutty Sark* in dry dock. Traditional English fare with some extra river trimmings—whitebait suppers, also roast beef, ubiquitous steak and kidney pudding. *LD open to 22.00. Closed Sun, L Sat.* **£.**

Hispaniola   6 L 23

The Thames at Victoria Embankment, Charing Cross WC2. 01-839 3011. A restaurant floating on the Thames. Romantic setting. Good Spanish food on the upper or lower deck. Gazpacho, paella, prawns, seafood in white wine. Set menu. *LD (Reserve) open to 23.20. Sun to 21.50. Closed L Sat.* A.Ax.B.Cb.Dc. **£££.**

Kouzina

6 Vicarage Rd, Kingston upon Thames, Surrey. 01-546 1336. Friendly, cluttered restaurant just off the river. Large menu with a selection of English and Continental dishes. Far the best are the Greek specialities: afelia,

shashliks, tava—lamb in a wine sauce, sfoliatella—pancake with rosewater and chestnut purée. Greek music. *LD (Reserve D) open to 22.30. Closed Sun.* A.Ax.B.Dc. **££.**

London Apprentice

62 Church St, Old Isleworth, Middx. 01-560 3538. A 15th century Thames-side pub, with fine Elizabethan and Georgian interiors, decorated with prints of Hogarth's 'Apprentices'. The first floor restaurant overlooks the river and provides excellent English fare. Perhaps unadventurous but the established favourites are preferred here—white sole, roast duckling. *LD open to 21.00. Closed Sun, D Mon, L Sat.* A.B. **££.**

Mayflower

117 Rotherhithe St SE16. 01-237 4088. A 17th century pub overlooking the river; connected historically with the 'Mayflower' and early prints echo this theme. A collection of Pilgrim Fathers' implements and wooden church carvings. A true English menu, Mrs Beeton's fish pie, steaks, lamb cutlets—no trimmings, but cheerfully served and good value. *LD open to 21.30. Closed Sun, L Sat.* A.Ax.B.Dc. **££.**

National Theatre Restaurant   6 M 24

Upper Ground, South Bank SE1. 01-928 2033. An oblong-shaped restaurant on the first floor of the National Theatre complex. To get a good view of the river, it is necessary to book well in advance. Interesting collection of paintings bequeathed by Somerset Maugham. A predominantly English menu including roast Aylesbury duckling with orange salad, grilled trout with tarragon, spiced fillet of veal served with rice. Extensive wine list. Lunch on Saturdays only. *D (Reserve) open to 23.30. Closed Sun.* **££.**

Nautical Wheel

Wallingford, Oxon. Wallingford 36507. Boat-house restaurant on a deserted part of the Thames. Rather primitive facilities. But good boeuf bourguignonne, lamb in sour cream, veal marsala with olives and anchovies. Pineapple cheesecake to follow. *LD (Reserve) open to 20.30. Closed Mon, D Sun.* B. **££.**

Princes Room, Tower Hotel   6 R 32

St Katherine's Way E1. 01-481 2575. Pleasantly

situated hotel by St Katherine's Docks. Look out over the Thames and Tower Bridge from the windows of the cocktail bar and restaurant. International cuisine. Diced avocado with smoked salmon and prawns in a creamed horse-radish mayonnaise, fillet of sea bass cooked in artichoke purée, lettuce and cream, escalope de veau Western Isles, lamb cutlets coated with mushroom purée and foie gras and baked in a strudel pastry. To follow crêpes Suzettes or a straightforward selection of sweets. *LD (Reserve) open to 23.00. Sun to 22.30.* A.Ax.B.Cb.Dc. **£££.**

La Riva

Raymead Rd, Maidenhead, Berks. Maidenhead 33522. Small restaurant by Old Maidenhead Bridge, beside the Thames. Old-fashioned linen table-napkins and flowers. Varied Italian menu. Vichyssoise, costata alla pizzaiola, scallopine a la Riva. *LD (Reserve) open to 22.30. Closed Sun.* A.Ax.B.Dc. **££.**

Royal Festival Hall Restaurant   6 M 23

Royal Festival Hall, South Bank SE1. 01-928 2829. Large restaurant on the third level overlooking the Thames. Pre-concert set meal in the evening plus an à la carte menu. Riverside cafeteria downstairs. Across at the National Film Theatre there is also a small self-service restaurant with a view of the Thames. *LD open to 22.00. Closed Sun, L Sat.* A.Ax.B.Dc. **££.**

St George & Dragon Restaurant

Henley Rd, Wargrave, Berkshire. Wargrave 2815. French and English food in a pretty pub looking on to the river. Drink on the terrace in fine weather. English carvery, steaks, chicken chasseur, tournedos. *LD open to 21.30. Closed D Sun, L Mon.* A.Ax.B.Dc. **£.**

Samuel Pepys at Brooks Wharf   6 M 28

48 Upper Thames St EC4. 01-248 3048. Attractive traditional style with two large bars and an excellent restaurant. A two-tiered terrace overlooks the river and there is constant tickertape news from the wires of UNS and UPI on the staircase. Old lamps and prints hang on the walls, as well as some letters by the diarist himself. English fare—roast or sirloin beef, game pie and 'Spotted Dick' for afters. *LD (Reserve) open to 21.00. Fri & Sat. to 22.30. Closed L Sat.* A.Ax.B.Dc. **££.**

Trafalgar Tavern
Park Row SE10. 01-858 2437. Thames-side near Wren's Naval College. Cocktail lounge and one ground floor room with large windows overlooking the river. English menu with varying specialities. Whitebait for starters. Steak, kidney and oyster pie, saddle of venison, roast goose in cider sauce and Mermaid's Purse—puff pastry filled with different fish and broccoli. Wide selection of desserts. The original navigational instruments from the Tavern's namesake are displayed. *LD (Reserve) open to 21.45. Closed D Sun.* A.Ax.B.Dc. **££.**

Russian, Polish and Czechoslovakian

If you like fish—cold, hot, winey, spiced, salted—and particularly herrings (or caviar!) then try some of the restaurants listed below. You will find borscht (cold beetroot soup) and plenty of sour cream in beef Stroganoff. Blinis—savoury or sweet pancakes filled with everything from herrings to sour cream; piroghki—puff pastry pasties filled with fish or meat, eggs and onion; koulibiaki—filled with fresh salmon, herbs and rice. Try stuffed cabbage, veal in egg and breadcrumbs, and rice, used in moulds to hold together all sorts of fruity sweets and many kasha (grain and buckwheat) dishes.

Borshtch N'Tears   2 I 12
45 Beauchamp Place SW3. 01-589 5003. Crowded, informal restaurant popular with young people. Russian music played on the ground floor, rock music downstairs. Atmosphere can get very lively—it is not unknown to see people dancing on the tables. Try the borscht, beef Stroganoff, chicken Dragomirof—white wine, cream and gherkin sauce; golubtsy—stuffed cabbage leaves and blinis. Also a branch at 273 King's Rd SW3. 01-352 5786. *D open to 01.30.* A.Ax.B.Dc. **££.**

Daquise   1 I 9
20 Thurloe St SW7. 01-589 6117. Very popular with

Polish emigrés, this restaurant serves simple, inexpensive but very well prepared dishes. Borscht, stuffed cabbage, bigor and sausages, shaslik. Also open for morning coffee and afternoon tea when they serve some of the most delicious pastries in London. *LD open to 23.35.* **£.**

Luba's Bistro 1 I 11
6 Yeoman's Row SW3. 01-589 2950. Individual, down to earth, spartan atmosphere. Seating at long tables. Bring your own wine. View of the kitchen. But good wholesome Russian cooking at low prices. Borscht, beef Stroganoff, golubtsy, pojarsky. *LD open to 23.45. Closed Sun.* A.B. **£.**

Moravia 1 B 11
62 Queensway W2. 01-229 4199. Owned by Czechs and offering genuine Slav as well as Continental dishes. Small café/restaurant done up as a pseudo log cabin, complete with Czech folk songs throughout the evening

for entertainment. Varied menu: hot salt beef, goulash, sauerkraut, dumplings and Moravian sausage. Junipery Czech gin or beer. An unusual place; the bill won't break the bank either. *LD open to 24.00.* A.Ax.B.Dc. **££.**

Nikita's   4 J 4
65 Ifield Rd SW10. 01-352 6326. Russian dishes, slightly adapted to Western tastes. Small basement restaurant, quite pretty. Service helpful; willing to explain the cooking and give advice. Good selection of Russian vodka. *D (Reserve) open to 23.30. Closed Sun.* A.Ax.Dc. **£££.**

The Rasputin   2 I 19
50 Dover St W1. 01-493 7971. Split-level cellar restaurant offering good live entertainment and solid Russian food. To start, there is an authentic mixed hors d'oeuvres, borscht and piroshky, or smoked sturgeon. The latter can also be had grilled on skewers as a main course. Naturally, there is chicken Kiev and beef Stroganoff, but the more traditional boiled meat dumplings served in sour cream (plemeni) are definitely worth tasting. Resident band plays nightly from 21.00. Cossack, Caucasian, or Armenian dancers perform three times a week. Attentive service in a lively, White Russian atmosphere. *LD (Reserve) open to 01.00. Closed Sun, L Sat.* A.Ax.B.Cb.Dc. **£££.**

Scandinavian

Scandinavian food is above all healthy, with the emphasis on fresh, natural raw materials. It includes plenty of milk, cheese, fish, raw vegetables and rye bread. Sauces are kept simple. Smörgåsbord consists of rye bread decorated with pieces of cheese, herring, smoked salmon, beef or pork. Seafood features prominently on many menus; much of it is smoked, marinated, pickled or served with sour cream. Reindeer, mutton or whale meat can be eaten smoked or fresh. Hams, sausages and regional cheeses are delicious.

Anna's Place
90 Mildway Park N1. 01-249 9379. Anna and her brother run this small, intimate restaurant, popular with the inhabitants of Islington. Sited in her own home, Anna takes pleasure in describing the various dishes on the French and Scandinavian menu. For starters camembert with parsley has been highly praised followed by raw marinated salmon. Reasonable wine list. Essential to book. *D (Reserve) open to 22.15. Closed Sun, Mon.* **££.**

Hungry Viking   1 B 9
44 Ossington St W2. 01-727 3311. Small, welcoming authentic Scandinavian restaurant. Bar decorated with skis. The helpful waitresses wear national costume. Good cooking, fresh raw materials. Fixed price smögåsbord and a hot soup of the day. Good marinated fish. Schnapps to drink. *D open to 23.00. Closed Mon.* A.Ax.B.Dc. **££.**

Spanish and Portuguese

Spaniards are very fond of fish—whole baby eels, squid (calamares), salt cod with fresh tomatoes or fresh cod in olive oil and garlic (pil-pil). A typical meal in a Spanish restaurant might include 'gazpacho' a chilled soup of tomatoes, garlic, bread crumbs, green pepper, cucumber, oil and vinegar; then 'paella', a famous national dish of rice flavoured with saffron to which chicken or prawns, clams and squid are added. Zarzuela is fish stew and chorizo is a peppery red sausage often stewed with red beans.
Portuguese cooking is not as oily as Spanish. Some excellent soups are made with fish, hare and rabbit. Crayfish, stuffed crabs, prawns, cockles and shrimps are also served, as well as sole, bass, red mullet and fresh sardines. A delicacy is smoked swordfish. Smoked pig tongues are highly recommended, also 'cosido'—boiled bacon, sausages, rice and chick peas.

Alonso's   4 Q 11
32 Queenstown Rd SW8. 01-720 5986. Imaginative food; charming and efficient service. You have to ring a bell to get in. Rich red decor and dim lights. The

cooking is a mixture of styles, the menu table d'hôte. Gazpacho, prawns in hot sauce, champagne and camembert soup, chicken stuffed with apricots and avocado, lobster. To follow, oranges in Grand Marnier, cold caramel and apple soufflé. *LD (Reserve D) open to 23.30. Closed Sun, L Sat.* Ax.Dc. **££.**

Barcelona Restaurant 2 H 20
17 Beak St W1. 01-734 6615. Step inside away from the bustle of central London and you will find yourself in an intimate, authentic Spanish atmosphere. Heavy dark brown wood furnishings, whitewashed walls, alcoves and booths—all give credence to the Iberian feeling in the restaurant. Full range of Spanish specialities: gazpacho, avocado Maria Luisa, paella, tortillas, zarzuela (mixed sea-food cooked in brandy), grilled Mediterranean prawns, entrecôte Garate served with asparagus and mushroom sauce. A guitarist plays nightly. *LD open to 24.00.* A.Ax.B. **££.**

El Bodegon 4 L 6
9 Park Walk SW10. 01-352 1330. Intimate, cool and popular. Mainly Spanish dishes, excellently cooked. Gambas al pil-pil (prawns in a hot garlic sauce), envuelta (breast of chicken with pâté and ham, rolled in pastry and served in champagne sauce). Good value set lunch. *LD open to 24.00.* A.Ax.B.Cb.Dc. **££.**

Fogareiro
16 Hendon Lane N3. 01-346 0315. Senor Costa has given his restaurant a distinctly marine decor to match the emphasis on fish specialities in his popular Portuguese menu. The walls of the three small rooms are covered in fishing nets, there is rope all around and the lighting is cleverly arranged in life buoys. Try the sea-food pancake flamed in brandy to start. A typically Portuguese main dish might be king prawns piri-piri (very hot and spicy), lagosta suada (fresh lobster cooked in olive oil, tomatoes, onions, herbs and port) or diced steak fried in herbs and garlic. Considerate service. *LD (Reserve) open to 23.30. Closed Sun.* A.Ax.B.Dc. **££.**

Martinez 2 I 20
25 Swallow St W1. 01-734 5066. Rather luxurious old-fashioned Spanish restaurant. Pre-dinner sherry bar for

apéritifs, then ascend a curved and gracious staircase to the dining room. Wall tiles and thick carpets. An international and Spanish menu. Garlic soup with egg, calamares en su tinta (baby octopus cooked in their own sauce), zarzuela (fish and shell fish soup), kidneys in sherry and a variety of paellas. Guitarist in the evenings. Courteous service. *LD (Reserve) open to 23.15. Sun to 22.30.* A.Ax.B.Dc. **££**.

O Fado   2 I 12
50 Beauchamp Place SW3. 01-589 3002. A genuine Portuguese restaurant with music in the basement. Delicious fish cooked in many different ways. Sardines and the chicken speciality—franquintos a Fado—are superb. Good carafe wine. *D open to 00.30. Sun to 23.30.* **££**.

Swiss

Swiss cookery is wholesome and unfanciful. 'Fondue' is a concoction of cheese—usually emmental or gruyère—melted and mixed with garlic, white wine and Kirsch. It is brought bubbling to the table and eaten by dipping morsels of French bread into the pot. It is not advisable to drink anything but wine, Kirsch, tea or coffee with such a meal. 'Kassupe' is a cheese soup and 'croûte au fromage' is a tasty Swiss version of Welsh rarebit. Also worth trying are country cured pork meats. And the pâtisserie—cakes and pastries with mountains of fresh cream—are of course delicious.

St Moritz   2 I 21
161 Wardour St W1. 01-734 3324. Typical Swiss decor with wooden panels, beams, cowbells and the first floor rigged out like a ski hut in the famous resort. Cheese and beef fondues are a house speciality. Also assiette de grison (mountain-air dried and cured beef), Berner platte, which incorporates smoked ham, pork, sauerkraut, beans, potato, boiled beef, sausage and knodels, and sliced veal in cream and mushroom sauce served with authentic Rosti potatoes. For dessert: pineapple and Swiss Kirsch. *LD (Reserve) open to 01.00. Sun to 23.30. Closed L Sat, L Sun.* A.Ax.B.Cb.Dc. **££**.

The Swiss Centre   **2 I 22**
1 New Coventry St (Leicester Square) W1. 01-734
1291. Large restaurant complex comprising five venues
at different price ranges serving Swiss provincial food.
The **Chesa** is the most up-market, with rough white
walls and heavy wooden partitions. The menu is varied
with international as well as Swiss dishes. The **Rendez-
Vous** emphasises Swiss-German cuisine including
steaks and light meals. The **Taverne** has a warmer
atmosphere where you can enjoy various cheese dishes
and regional sausages. The **Locanda**, as its name
suggests, offers Swiss-Italian cooking with a special
'business lunch' and some freshly made pasta dishes.
Finally, the **Swiss Imbiss** opens every day for breakfast
and carries on throughout the day serving coffee,
chocolate croissants, flans and snacks. Pleasant light
Swiss wines available. *LD open to 24.00*.
A.Ax.B.Cb.Dc. **£—£££.**

Thai

Thai cuisine is rich and highly seasoned with pounded
chillies and spices. Rice and fish predominate, and
many recipes include 'Nam Pla' a salty fish sauce.
Exotic vegetables, flowers and blossoms are often
served raw and dipped into a sauce. Presentation is very
important. All food is exquisitely arranged, often cut
into delicate shapes. Thai salads such as rose petal or
water chestnut are recommended. Most dishes,
including soups, are eaten all at once, and not served
separately, as in the West. Thai desserts which include
lotus seeds, ming beans, cassava roots and coconut are
often scented with jasmin and other aromatic flowers.

Bangkok   **1 I 9**
9 Bute St SW7. 01-584 8529. Simple spick and span
dining room. Portions are rather small. Try the beef
satay in peanut sauce, Thai noodles, chicken fried in
garlic or prepared with ginger. *LD (Reserve) open to
22.45. Closed Sun.* **£.**

Busabong   **4 L 4**
331 Fulham Rd SW1. 01-352 4742. On two floors, set

menu upstairs, where you are expected to sit on the floor. Thai dancers perform downstairs in the more formal surroundings. A la carte menu. Very pleasant, attentive service. Fisherman's soup, satay beef in a delicate peanut sauce, mint pork with minced water chestnuts covered in wun tun sauce. To follow Thai egg custards, coconut banana. *LD (Reserve) open to 23.00.* A.Ax.Dc. **££.**

Siam
1 F 7

12 St Alban's Grove W8. 01-937 8765. Authentic Thai establishment on two floors. Sumptuous dining room downstairs to enjoy native dancing and listen to Thai music. Menu is changed daily; noodles with coconut juice and pineapple, barbecued beef satay, chicken fried with pepper and garlic. Jasmin tea or wine. Delicate, helpful service. *LD (Reserve D) open to 23.00. Closed L Sat, L Mon.* Ax.B.Dc. **££.**

Thai Restaurant
1 D 4

209 Kensington High St W8. 01-937 2260. Basement restaurant, simple Thai-style decor with an interesting glass cabinet displaying theatre masks, swords and dolls. Daily specialities such as sweet and sour chicken curry, steamed fish with soya beans and ginger, fried rainbow trout in pink sauce. Various fried noodle dishes called Phad Thai. Try Med Kanon (jak fruit seeds) or Kanon-Tua-Paet (green beans with coconut, sesame and sugar) for dessert. *LD (Reserve) open to 22.30.* A.Ax.B.Dc. **£.**

Unusual eating

Beefeater
6 R 33

Ivory House, St Katherine's Dock E1. 01-408 1001. Suitably situated near the Tower of London, here Henry VIII and his court provide dancing and entertainment. But take care to hold on to your head! No eating utensils are given with the five course medieval-style dinner. Bread and pâté, soup, fish, chicken and fresh fruit. Unlimited wine, beer and mead flows. *D (Reserve) open to 23.30.* A.Ax.B.Cb.Dc. **£££+.**

Blitz 3 I 24
4 Great Queen St WC2. 01-405 6598. A World War II theme dominates this extremely popular London night spot. The place is decorated with British Rail posters and newspaper cuttings from the period. Upstairs, there is an à la carte menu offering schnitzels, plaice, trout, hamburgers, kebabs, steaks and chicken Kiev. Downstairs, there is a cocktail bar and disco most nights, with a cabaret three times a week. The emphasis tends to be on modern visually exciting groups or jazz bands. The atmosphere is informal and very gay. *LD (Reserve) open to 01.00. Closed L Sat, L Sun.* **£.**

Caledonian Suite 2 G 20
Hanover St W1. 01-408 1001. Starting with a whisky reception, enjoy a Scottish evening complete with bagpipes, cabaret and 'ceremony of the haggis'. Kilts are provided for gentlemen who prefer skirts! The five course meal includes Scotch broth, escalope with shrimps and prawns, haggis, roast beef and sherry trifle. Drink as much wine and beer as you want. Dancing. *D (Reserve) open to 24.00.* A.Ax.B.Cb.Dc. **£££+.**

Cockney Cabaret 2 I 22
18 Charing Cross Rd WC2. 01-408 1001. Music hall entertainment in traditional East End style. Dancing, production numbers and comic acts. Honky tonk piano greets you at the whisky and gin reception. Cockney 'nosh' to follow—vegetable soup, chicken, fish, apple pie and custard. Free flowing wine and beer. *D (Reserve) open to 24.00.* A.Ax.B.Cb.Dc. **£££+.**

Flanagan's
100 Baker St W1. 01-935 0287 2 C 18
9 Kensington High St W8. 01-937 2519. 1 D 4
Completely phoney but enjoyable Victorian dining rooms, with sawdust for spitting on, stalls, cockney songs and colourful extravaganza. Elegantly costumed waiters and serving girls; ideal place to entertain silent or difficult guests. The pianist slams his piano at you, and the waitresses sing as do the customers. Tripe, jellied eels, game pie, enormous plates of fish and chips, and golden syrup pudding. *LD open to 23.15.* A.Ax.B.Cb.Dc. **££.**

Gallipoli 6 N 32
8 Bishopsgate Churchyard EC2. 01-588 1922. Exotic and unusual, away from the West End; once a Turkish bath, with original gold decor and tiles—now a night-club restaurant with twice nightly cabaret of fascinating belly dancing. Excellent Turkish food. Shish kebab, buryan Gallipoli, red mullet. Also some international dishes. Twenty-dish choice of hors d'oeuvres. *LD (Reserve) open to 03.00. Closed Sun. Cabaret 22.30 & 01.00*. A.Ax.B.Cb.Dc. **£££**.

Sailing Junk 1 F 6
59 Marloes Rd W8. 01-937 2589. A romantic family concern of Mr Looi. Float through the ten-course Dragon Festival dinner in an old Chinese sailing junk, candles flickering and soft Mandarin music piping. Food is a mixture of Cantonese and Pekinese. The special Steamboat soup—chicken, lettuce, bamboo shoots and water chestnuts—is cooked at the table. *D (Reserve weekends) open to 23.30*. A.Ax. B.Dc. **££**.

Shakespeare's Tavern and Playhouse 6 L 27
Blackfriars Lane EC4. 01-248 9955. Boisterous evening with Shakespearian cabaret, court jesters, puppet show and conga dancing. Five course set meal, duck and orange pâté, cream of watercress soup, deep fried fish, roast chicken and vegetables, apple pie and cream. Plenty of wine, beer, cider and mead. The restaurant itself is situated in vast old wine cellars. Disco dancing too if you have the energy. *D (Reserve) open to 24.00. Closed Tue & Thur in winter*. A.Ax.B.Cb.Dc. **£££**.

Tudor Rooms 5 J 22
80 St Martins Lane WC2. 01-240 3978. Jesters and troubadours entertain you while you eat a five course meal in the style of 'Olde Englande', served by buxom wenches. You are liable to get put in the stocks and pelted with bread. You simply have to like jollity, vulgarity and togetherness to enjoy it. Two international acts as well. Specialities include old English beef not roast but stewed. *D (Reserve) open to 02.00*. A.Ax.B.Cb.Dc. **££**.

Villa dei Cesari   5 Q 15
135 Grosvenor Rd SW1. 01-828 7453. Converted
riverside warehouse with a fine view over the Thames.
The Roman Empire lives on here: classical decor,
Latinised menu and waiters in tunics. Dancing to
resident band. *D open to 02.30. Closed Mon.* Ax.B.Dc.
£££.

Vegetarian and wholefood

These places serve mainly imaginative mixed salads,
quiches, pulses, savouries and curries. Some provide a
small meat menu. Many people eat in them for religious
reasons, others because it's healthy and reputedly less
fattening. Prices are not rock bottom, but the queues
are evidence of popularity and good value. The
majority of the restaurants are buffet service. Wine is
not always available.

Baba Bhelpoori House
118 Westbourne Grove W2. 01-271 7502. Neat, clean
and simple decor. A tasty blend of western and
southern Indian vegetarian dishes. Dosa (pancake filled
with lentils and coconut chutney), thali (a set meal
including a starter, two vegetable dishes, chapatis, rice
and a sweet). An interesting range of Bombay sea-side
snacks. For dessert try Shrikand—yoghurt with
saffron, almonds, pistacchio and sugar. *LD open to
23.00. Closed Mon.* **£.**

Beverley Vegetarian Restaurant   2 F 18
24–25 Binney St W1. 01-629 7123. One of the oldest
established vegetarian restaurants in London. Has a
large seating capacity for Oxford St shoppers. All the
food is freshly prepared each day, including the yoghurt
which is made on the premises. Try their excellent
mushroom pie, potatoes sautéd with onions and cheese
or vegetable goulash. To follow either home-made
chocolate sponge, apricot tart or fresh fruit muesli.
Unlicensed. *L open to 16.00. Closed Sat & Sun.* **£.**

Cranks   2 H 21
8 Marshall St W1. 01-437 9431. Also in Heals,
Tottenham Court Rd. Light and pleasant atmosphere

in this popular, self-service vegetarian restaurant. Very crowded, especially at lunchtime. Vegetable dishes, nut and vegetable loaf, salads; muesli and fruit pies. Also an excellent juice bar serving yoghurts and fresh fruit juices. *LD open to 20.30. Sat. to 16.30. Closed Sun.* **£.**

Di's Larder
62 Lavender Hill SW11. 01-223 4613. Relaxing atmosphere in this small wholefood shop and restaurant. The three owners used to work in the theatre and they try quite successfully to provide an imaginative menu, nicely prepared and courteously served. Vegetarian moussaka, tabbouleh salad, courgettes in cream, mushrooms and wine, quiches, hot pizzas, stuffed aubergines. Good choice of breads baked on the premises: milk loaf, plain whole wheat, sesame whole wheat and granary. Herb teas and fresh fruit juices. *LD open to 19.00. Closed Sun.* **£.**

Earth Exchange
213 Archway Rd N6. 01-340 6407. Run as a collective with a book and herb shop on the first floor, a wholefood shop on the ground floor and a café in the basement. Although there is no set menu, a vegan dish is always available as are salads, quiches, pizzas and fruit crumbles. The vegetables are organically grown and no refined sugar is used. An ethnic, homey atmosphere with many of the main dishes relying on inspiration rather than expertise. *LD open to 18.30. Fri, Sat & Sun to 21.30. Closed Wed & Thur.* **£.**

Food for Thought   3 I 23
31 Neal St WC2. 01-836 0239. Simple, whitewashed Covent Garden restaurant, catering for about 40 people. Not a large menu but the food is home-grown: compost grown vegetables, free-range eggs. Home-made soups, vegetable stews, chick pea casserole, vegetarian bakes, quiches and a selection of tasty salads. To follow yoghurt, fruit salads or an assortment of cakes. Drink tisanes or bring your own wine. *LD open to 20.00. Closed Sat & Sun.* **£.**

Highways Vegetarian Restaurant   2 F 20
Roxburghe House (lower ground floor), 273–287 Upper Regent St W1. 01-629 5389. Very long established self-service vegetarian restaurant with a

regular and loyal clientele. Here, decor is unimportant as all concentration is focused on the food. Stuffed pimentos, ratatouille, cheese soufflé, flans, stuffed pancakes, stuffed marrow and cauliflower cheese are among the daily hot and cold dishes. Good fresh fruit juices. A place to remember in the heart of 'junk food' London. *L open to 15.00. Closed Sat & Sun.* £.

Mandeer   2 G 22

21 Hanway Place W1. 01-323 0660. Kitchen is on view to the diners in this popular vegetarian restaurant. It certainly deserves its good reputation, as the food is cooked to a very high standard. A word of warning, all the curries are strongly spiced. Specialities include aubergine bhajias, thali Mandeer or puffed lotus savoury. *LD open to 22.15. Closed Sun.* A. Ax. £.

Manna

4 Erskine Rd NW3. 01-722 8028. Good, reliable food in this authentic vegetarian restaurant. Cool stone floors and massive pine tables help to create a farmhouse kitchen atmosphere. All the food is made on the premises, including yoghurts and bread. Spinach pancakes, hizki-seaweed and vegetable casserole, celery and apple salad with curd cheese. A choice of wine or organic cider. *D open to 23.45. Closed Mon.* £.

Nuthouse   2 H 20

26 Kingly St W1. 01-437 9471. Self-service restaurant on two floors with a take-away service for Carnaby St shoppers in a hurry. The food is all organically grown and freshly cooked. Macrobiotic dishes are also available. Nut rissoles, nut roast and a different salad everyday. To follow fruit crumble and yoghurt. To drink either wine, fresh fruit juice or herb teas. *L open to 17.00. Closed Sat & Sun.* £.

Oodles

3 Fetter Lane EC4. 01-353 1984.   6 K 26
L open to 15.00. Closed Sat & Sun.
113 High Holborn WC1. 01-405 3838.   3 I 23
LD open to 19.00. Closed Sun, D Sat.
42 New Oxford St W1. 01-580 9521.   3 H 23
LD open to 20.00. Sun to 19.00.
31 Cathedral Place EC4. 01-248 2550.   6 L 28
L open to 17.00. Closed Sat & Sun.

Not strictly a vegetarian chain of restaurants, although they offer a wide variety of vegetable dishes and salads. The food is standardised and can sometimes be over-cooked. Always crowded at lunchtime. Try their savour flans, leeks au gratin or their distinctive aubergine ragoût. Wine can be bought by the glass. **£.**

Oodles   **2 D** 16
128 Edgware Rd W2. 01-723 7548. No longer part of the chain, this restaurant was bought by a former area manager of Oodles and his partner. Run on similar lines to the chain they offer the same variety of food although the standard is generally higher. *LD open to 21.00. Sun to 20.00.* **£.**

Raw Deal   **2 B** 17
65 York St W1. 01-262 4841. Self-service restaurant. Unlicensed but you may bring your own bottle.

Organically grown vegetables when possible. Risottos, savoury pancake, stuffed vegetables, a splendid variety of salad dishes and quiches. To follow pies, cakes and trifles—all made on the premises from wholemeal flour. *LD open to 22.00. Sat to 23.00. Closed Sun.* **£.**

Sharuna 3 H 23

107 Gt Russell St WC1. 01-636 5922. Authentic Indian vegetarian dishes. Specialities include savoury doughnuts with yoghurt and Bombay Special—for those who like very hot chilli sauce. Delicious sweets to follow. Licensed, but try their sweet or salt lassi with your meal. *LD open to 21.45. Sun to 21.00.* A.B.Dc. **£.**

Slenders 6 L 28

41 Cathedral Place EC4. 01-236 5974. Situated in the modern square by St Paul's Cathedral. Bright and airy with pine tables and hessian walls. Delicious home-made soups, vegetable casserole and flans. To follow a wide selection of cakes such as apple pie or meringue. *LD open to 18.15. Closed Sat & Sun.* **£.**

Sunwheel Café

3 Chalk Farm Rd NW1. 01-267 8116. A macrobiotic restaurant also offering fish and some specialities with an oriental influence. Falafal, deep fried bean curd, six different salads, beanburgers and an interesting variety of sea vegetables. There is usually a soup and fish of the day. Poached cod or mackerel with miso tahini sauce. Try carob cake made from natural chocolate or tofu (bean curd) cream cake to follow. The place is pleasingly decorated in cream and brown with matching table-cloths. High-backed chairs with straw seats are complemented by the straw lamp shades. Live music five nights a week, both classical and jazz. Licensed. *LD (Reserve D) open to 20.30. Sat & Sun to 21.30. Closed Mon.* **£.**

Vijay

49 Willesden Lane NW6. 01-328 1087. Traditional south Indian vegetarian food served here as well as tasty meat curries for any non-vegetarian friends you might bring along. Try their masala dosai, sambar or vegetables cooked in yoghurt and coconut. To follow genuine Indian sweets—almond cakes. *LD (Reserve D) open to 22.45.* **£.**

Wholefood Farm Bar   **2 D** 18
110 Baker St W1. 01-486 8444. High quality health
food restaurant. Everything is grown naturally—
organic vegetables, free-range chickens; the meat is free
from any injections. Lentil soup, artichoke and leek
crumble, shepherds pie, ham and roast beef and a
selection of different salads. To follow, flap-jacks, fresh
fruit, caraway seed cake. Also serve breakfasts. *LD
open to 20.00. Sat to 15.00. Closed Sun in winter*. Dc.
£.

Wholemeal Café
1 Shrubbery Rd, Streatham SW16. 01-769 2423. A
fresh rustic atmosphere with plain brick walls, wooden
furnishing, stringed ceiling and a brown and green
colour scheme. Home-made soups, salads, various
quiches and pizzas. Strictly vegetarian. Usually two hot
dishes of the day—a stew, curry or casserole. Various
bakes and broccoli or cauliflower in a cheese and
tomato sauce. Red and white house wine. Fresh juices,
herb teas and barley cup. Oat cakes, short-breads, hot
puddings or a delicious yoghurt with fruit, nuts and
honey for dessert. No smoking allowed. *LD open to
18.00. Fri & Sat to 22.00*. **£**.

West Indian

West Indian cooking is a mixture that has accrued from
all the various peoples who have lived there: African,
English, French, Spanish—all based on locally
available produce. The dishes are characterised by the
use of pungent spices and peppers and are very
colourful. Coconut and exotic fruits are much in
evidence as is fish and seafood which is a staple of the
Caribbean diet.

La Caraibe   **4 O** 1
182 Wandsworth Bridge Rd SW6. 01-731 0732. One of
London's newest Caribbean restaurants specialising in
Creole-style cuisine from Martinique, Guadeloupe and
Dominica. Two pleasantly decorated rooms, ground
floor and basement, linked by a wrought iron spiral
staircase. Tropical plants abound and a conservatory

houses banana and coconut trees. To start, try Callaloo soup, made from taro leaves or spinach, with okra, smoked pork, crab, coconut milk and spices; also Avocado Diabolo—filled with salted cod, garlic, tomatoes, hot peppers and lime juice. Choice of six main courses: specially recommended is Poul à la creme Coco, chicken cooked in coconut, nutmeg and spices, or pork stuffed with bacon, ham, chicken and olives, served with Calypso sauce. Exciting vegetables—dasheen, yams, sweet potatoes, breadfruit, christothin. For dessert, sample the banana dishes, ginger mousse, or the fresh West Indian fruit salad. Buffet lunch on Sunday in summer months. *LD open to 23.30. Closed Sun.* **££.**

Ocho Rios Room   2 B 16
22 Harcourt St W1. 01-262 3369. Bertie Greene's authentic Jamaican restaurant dispenses with any trimmings—not the smartest place, a plain simple room with small tables and infrequently laundered table cloths. Yet the cocktails will put you in an excellent frame of mind. An interesting menu; rich gungo pea soup, stuffed puss prayers (avocado filled with salt fish), spicy pineapple roast duck, crab in sweet pepper sauce, chicken creole. To follow, baked bananas and rum sauce, mango and sweet pancakes. Aromatic coffee to end the meal. Jamaican recorded music. *LD (Reserve) open to 22.45. Closed Sun.* B. **££.**

Wine bars

In recent years, numerous wine bars have sprung up throughout London. They provide a relaxed, subdued, often candle-lit setting, where you can unwind and eat, drink wine and listen to music. Food normally consists of a large selection of cheeses, pâtés and salads. *Wine bars close at 23.00, unless otherwise stated.*

Balls Brothers
Eight wine bars in the City, one in the Strand and their venture in Chelsea make up this vastly popular chain. They share a common list of more than 60 wines, with the occasional fine claret or well chosen Burgundy. A

dozen wines by the glass include Beaujolais Villages, the house Chablis, and lesser growths from Alsace and the Loire. Food and its availability vary from bar to bar, from sandwiches to full restaurant meals. *LD open Mon–Fri to 19.30. Closed Sat & Sun.*

31 Cheyne Walk SW3. 01-352 4989.	**4 M**	8
142 Strand WC2. 01-836 0156.	**6 K**	23
2 Old Change Court, St Paul's Churchyard EC4. 01-248 8697.	**6 M**	28
3 Budge Row, Cannon St EC4. 01-248 7557.	**6 N**	29
Laurence Pountney Hill EC4. 01-283 2947.	**6 O**	23
42 Threadneedle St EC2. 01-283 6701.	**6 N**	31
St Mary at Hill EC3. 01-626 0321.	**6 P**	31
6 Cheapside EC2. 01-248 2708.	**6 M**	29
5 Carey Lane EC2. 01-606 4787.	**6 L**	29
Moor House, London Wall EC2. 01-628 3944.	**6 L**	31

Bill Bentley's   2 I 12

31 Beauchamp Place SW3. 01-589 5080. This converted house in a modish street offers a useful choice with its basement bistro, ground floor bar and seafood restaurant upstairs. Sherry, port, Madeira and a dozen wines by the glass; also about 40 well chosen bottles. Good red and white Burgundy, fine claret. Alsace, Loire and Rhone wines available, all bottled at their place of origin. Pleasant little garden for summer drinking. *LD. Closed Sun.*

Bill Bentley's   2 D 18

239 Baker St NW1. 01-935 3130. This agreeable traditionally decorated bar leads into a panelled restaurant with a formal menu. Downstairs is another bar serving simpler food, chiefly salads and terrines. Shares a list of well selected French and German wines with the Beauchamp Place branch—about 40 bottles from the principal areas, with another dozen by the glass. *LD. Closed Sun.*

Boos   2 A 18

1 Glentworth St NW1. 01-935 3827. Run by a husband and wife team, this pleasant mock Tudor wine bar is a haunt for wine lovers. Plenty of good bottles from France, Germany and Spain. Home-made soups, sandwiches, quiches and taramasalata. *LD open to 20.30. Closed Sat & Sun.*

Bow Wine Vaults 6 M 29

10 Bow Churchyard EC4. 01-248 1121. A handsome high-ceiling'd bar with two counters, justly popular for its sandwiches and first class cheeses. Splendid list of about a hundred fine wines, representative and carefully chosen, complements a choice of a dozen sound wines by the glass. Also sherry, port and malt whisky. Simple restaurant meals in the cellar at lunchtime only. *L open Mon–Fri to 14.30. Closed Sat & Sun.*

Brahms & Liszt 6 J 24

19 Russell St WC2. 01-240 3661. Lively addition to Covent Garden's revival. Upstairs and cellar bar. Music is rather loud, food varied, with the emphasis on cheeses and salads. Some hot dishes. Standard selection of wines. *LD Closed Sun.*

Coates 6 N 32

109 Old Broad St EC2. 01-628 2411. Also at 45 London Wall EC2. Two popular, long established City bars, mirrored and panelled, sharing the Corney and Barrow list as well as a distinctly masculine character. Short and variable list of wines by the glass, good sherry and port, and a great number of good bottles to drink or take away. Sandwiches and simple cold food. *LD open to 19.00. Closed Sat & Sun.*

Cork & Bottle 5 J 22

44–46 Cranbourne St WC2. 01-734 7807. Cellar bar just off Leicester Square run by two friendly young New Zealanders. Invariably packed. Twenty odd wines by the glass including some fine German bottles. Australian, Californian and South African wines are also stocked regularly. Interesting bin ends, sometimes unlisted, fairly priced. Exceptionally wide range of pâtés, mousses, cold meats, salads and cheeses. *LD. Closed Sun.*

Davy's

A group of wine bars with a distinctive house style, a compound of polished wood, sawdust floors, casks and boxes, cartoons, prints and pictures, pewter and brass, wine labels and old bottles. Equally consistent is the excellent cold table: ham off the bone, beef, game pies, crabs, prawns and smoked fish, usually a hot dish or two, game in season and good cheeses. Service shows old-fashioned standards of courtesy. Port, sherry and Madeira from the wood, sound French and German wines by the glass, fine wines by the bottle. The claret list is generally stronger than the Burgundy, but both exceptional and moderately priced. Particularly noteworthy are the blackboard special offers. These may include Montrose 1966. Palmer 1964 in half-bottles or Grande Marque champagne. *Open normal pub hours but the City bars close at 20.30. Some branches close at weekends—phone for details:*

Boot & Flogger   **6 Q** 27
10 Redcross Way SE1. 01-407 1184.

Bottlescrue   **6 K** 28
Bath House, Holborn Viaduct EC1. 01-248 2157.

Bung Hole   **3 I** 23
57 High Holborn WC1. 01-242 4318

City Boot   **6 L** 31
7 Moorfields High Walk, Moorgate EC2. 01-588 4766.

City Flogger   **6 O** 31
120 Fenchurch St EC3. 01-623 3251.

Davy's Wine Vaults
165 Greenwich High Rd SE10. 01-858 7204.

Gyngleboy   **2 B** 13
27 Spring St W2. 01-723 3351.

Mother Bunch's   **6 L** 28
Old Seacoal Lane EC4. 01-236 5317.

Skinkers   **6 Q** 30
38 Tooley St SE1. 01-407 9189.

Downs   2 I 17
5 Down St W1. 01-491 3810. Sleek Mayfair bar on two
levels with a lavish cold table downstairs. Hot dishes
too, and an interesting range of 25 or so wines by the
glass. Bottles are also well chosen. Some fine wines
from impeccable sources but unfortunately very highly
priced. Service variable. Music evenings only. *LD open
to 01.00 Mon–Sat. Sun to 24.00*.

Downstairs Wine Bar   2 I 13
Basil St Hotel, 8 Basil St SW3. 01-730 3411. Smartly
decorated basement bar in sharp contrast with the staid
elegance of the rest of the hotel. Enterprising and varied
food, largely Mediterranean. Standard choice of wines
by glass and bottle. A useful address for Knightsbridge
shoppers. *LD. Closed Sun*.

Ebury Wine Bar   5 M 13
139 Ebury St SW1. 01-730 5447. Cramped and
crowded but a pleasant place with an interesting list of
about 50 bottles. Some uncommon regional wines,
about 15 by the glass, and port and sherry from the
wood. Popular restaurant with steaks and chops, a cold
table, cheeses and English puddings. *LD*.

Heath's
34 Rosslyn Hill NW3. 01-435 5203. Live music every
night at this crowded, French café-like wine bar. Wide
range of medium-priced wines from France, Germany,
Italy, Yugoslavia and Hungary. Good choice of home-
cooked food: goulash, casseroles, plenty of pâtés,
cheeses and salamis. The house speciality is noodle
mince. Fresh Greek bread. *LD. Closed L Sun*.

Jimmie's Vinothèque   1 D 8
Kensington Church St W8. 01-937 9988. Long bar in
part of the old Kensington Barracks, appropriately
owned by a former Guards officer. Good grills, sound
house wines and a list notable for its fine claret. Very
popular, with live music in the evenings. *LD*.

Loose Box   2 I 12
7 Cheval Place SW7. 01-584 9280. Still owned by
Searcy's and entered at night through the Brompton
Road shop. A large wine bar on two floors, the food
more elaborate upstairs. Drinking list of no great
distinction, but a wide choice of modest bottles from

Spain and Portugal as well as France and Germany. Always packed, a very lively meeting place. Not the ideal spot for a quiet drink. *LD open to 21.15. Closed Sun.*

Motcomb's 5 J 14
26 Motcomb St SW1. 01-235 6382. Smartly decorated, as befits its address. Good sandwiches and cheeses upstairs, a restaurant proper in the basement. Usually a dozen or so wines by the glass and some worthwhile bottles. Disappointingly, the list is often not a reliable indication of what is available. *LD. Closed Sat & Sun.*

Penny's Place 6 J 23
6 King St WC2. 01-836 4553. Authentic Covent Garden look to this converted pub. The building dates back to 1660. Penny has tried to create a French ambience inside with a predominantly French wine list of over 46 labelled bottles. Also brandy, sherry, calvados, Yugoslavian, Spanish, Italian and a few German wines. Excellent cuisine in the cellar bistro. There is a cordon bleu chef on the premises who prepares a different menu every day. Dishes may include: garlic mushrooms, whitebait, liver in orange and white wine sauce, coq au vin, a selection of quiches. Live music every Friday night. *LD. Closed Sun.*

Shampers 2 H 20
4 Kingly St W1. 01-437 1692. Always a congenial atmosphere here and a very fine selection of wines. More than a dozen wines by the glass. At least 20 champagnes, vintage port, sherries, a whole range of vermouths, good clarets. Wines from Italy, France, Germany and Chile—the house wine is a French-bottled Burgundy. Delicious cold buffet on the ground floor: many cheeses, salads, home-made terrine with hollandaise and tomato sauce, cold rabbit in wine. Informal waitress service downstairs at lunch when some reliable hot food is available. Flamenco guitarist three times a week, otherwise baroque taped music or French pop. *LD (Reserve L). Closed Sat & Sun.*

Slatters 5 J 21
3 Panton St SW1. 01-839 4649. A very civilised cellar wine bar just off Leicester Square. Chocolate brown decor, cane-backed chairs and the signed prints by Tom

Merrifield are for sale. Extensive wine list including clarets, hocks, moselles, rosés and some excellent French white wine. When drinking the house wine, the bottle is put on your table and you are only charged for what is imbibed. First-rate cheeseboard, several varieties of quiches and salad, avocado with prawns, pâtés and two special hot dishes of the day. Classical music is played all the time. *LD. Closed Sun.*

Sloane's Wine Bar   **5 L** 12
51 Sloane Sq SW1. 01-730 4275. Large, candle-lit cellar bar beside the Royal Court Theatre. Standard selection of wines improved by some imaginative home-cooked food. Varied cheeseboard. Live music evenings. *LD.*

Tracks   **2 H** 22
Soho Square W1. 01-439 2318. Warm, modern decor. Pine furnishings, plants and paintings. There is also a stylish terrace for outside drinking in the summer. The wines are mainly French with a sprinkling of Italian bottles. Nicely presented cold buffet and a few hot dishes. As a bonus, breakfast and afternoon teas are served as well. *LD open to 24.00.*

El Vino   **6 K** 26
47 Fleet St EC4. 01-353 6786. Something of an institution; musty atmosphere and thoroughly masculine. Little seems to change here; still a regular haunt of male lawyers and journalists—women are traditionally not served at the bar. Spirits and liqueurs are available, also a wide range of Burgundy—red and white, claret—London and château bottled, a long list of German wines, and about 10 varieties of champagne very moderately priced. Sandwiches at lunchtime. A restaurant downstairs where it is essential to book. *LD open Mon–Fri to 20.00. Sat L only. Closed Sun.*

Whittington's   **6 N** 29
21 College Hill EC4. 01-248 5855. Handsome vaulted cellars, claimed once to have belonged to Sir Richard, makes an appealing wine bar on the fringe of the City. Enterprising menu—kipper pâté, taramosalata, chops, steaks, pies and salads—and a wide ranging list. Interesting regional wines and good bottles from Duboeuf and Jaboulet Vercherre. *Open L only. Closed Sat & Sun.*

Late night eating

The following restaurants, cafés and take-aways operate late, if not all night. Note that hotel coffee bars often operate a 24-hr service.

Calamitees
104 Heath St NW3. 01-435 2145. Hamburgers. *Open Mon–Thur to 01.30. Fri–Sun to 03.30.*

Canton Chinese Restaurant　　　　　　**2 I** 22
11 Newport Place WC2. 01-437 8935. *Open 24 hrs.*

Far East　　　　　　　　　　　　　　**2 I** 22
13 Gerrard St W1. 01-4376148. Chinese. *Open to 05.00.*

The Grecian　　　　　　　　　　　　**2 G** 22
27a Percy St W1. 01-636 6351. Greek. *Open to 03.00.*

Lido　　　　　　　　　　　　　　　　**2 I** 22
41 Gerrard St W1. 01-437 4431. Chinese. *Open to 04.30.*

Mike's Diner　　　　　　　　　　　　**2 H** 20
3 New Burlington St W1. 01-734 3075. Hamburgers and Continental specialities. *Open to 05.00.*

Rodos　　　　　　　　　　　　　　　**3 H** 23
59 St Giles High St WC2. 01-836 3177. Greek. *Open to 05.00.*

Snack Express　　　　　　　　　　　**2 H** 22
23 Greek St W1. 01-734 6889. Grills and hamburgers. *Open to 05.00.*

Toddies Restaurant　　　　　　　　　**1 I**　7
241 Old Brompton Rd SW5. 01-373 8217. English and African, also serves breakfast. *Open to 07.00. Closed Mon.*

Up All Night　　　　　　　　　　　　**4 L**　4
325 Fulham Rd SW10. 01-352 1998. Steaks, hamburgers, spaghetti and coffee. *Open to 06.00.*

Wimpy Bars
27 London St W2. 01-723 4721.　　　　　**2 B** 13
190 Shaftesbury Avenue WC2. 01-836 1194.　**2 I** 21
Hamburgers. *Open 24 hrs.*

Witchity's　　　　　　　　　　　　　**1 D**　4
253 Kensington High St W8. 01-937 2654. Steaks, hamburgers, Continental cuisine and breakfast. *Open to 07.00.*

Wurst Max
75 Westbourne Grove W2. 01-229 3771. German sausages. *Open to 04.00.*

Page index

Area index

Sunday eating index

MAPS

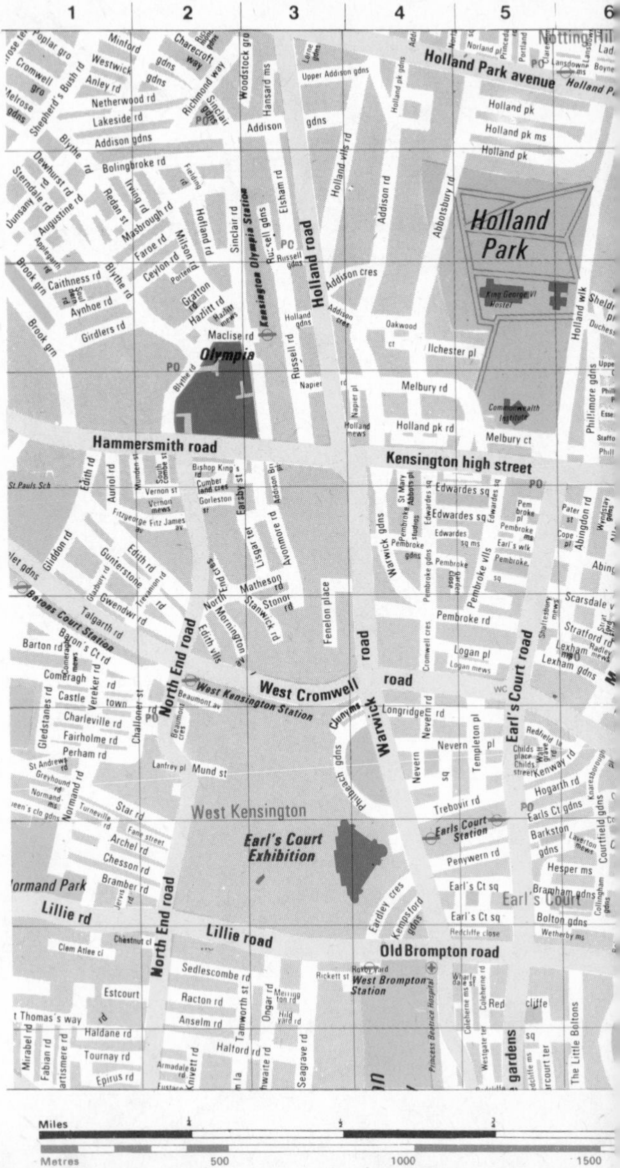
1
2
3
4
5
6
Holland Park avenue
Holland Park
King George VI Hostel
Commonwealth Institute
Hammersmith road
Kensington high street
Olympia
Kensington Olympia Station
Holland road
Addison cres
Addison gdns
Addison rd
Holland vils rd
Abbotsbury rd
Holland pk
Holland pk ms
Melbury rd
Melbury ct
Holland pk rd
Ilchester pl
Oakwood ct
Russell rd
Russell gdns
Elsham rd
Sinclair rd
Hansard ms
Woodstock gro
Upper Addison gdns
Minford gdns
Westwick gdns
Anley rd
Netherwood rd
Lakeside rd
Addison gdns
Blythe rd
Bolingbroke rd
Dewhurst rd
Sterndale rd
Dunsany rd
Augustine rd
Redan st
Irving rd
Masbrough rd
Faroe rd
Ceylon rd
Milson rd
Caithness rd
Aynhoe rd
Girdlers rd
Brook grn
Gratton rd
Hazlitt rd
Maclise rd
Shepherd's Bush rd
Richmond way
Charecroft way
Poplar gro
Cromwell gro
Melrose gdns
St Pauls Sch
Edith rd
Auriol rd
Munden st
Vernon st
Bishop King's rd
Gorleston st
Earsby st
Avonmore rd
Lisgar ter
Matheson rd
Stonor rd
North End cres
North End road
Edith vlls
Mornington av
Fenelon place
Gliddon rd
Gunterstone rd
Gwendwr rd
Talgarth rd
Barons Court Station
Baron's Ct rd
Barton rd
Comeragh rd
Castle town rd
Charleville rd
Fairholme rd
Perham rd
Gledstanes rd
Challoner st
Beaumont av
Beaumont cres
West Kensington Station
West Cromwell road
Warwick road
Warwick gdns
Clunymas
Philbeach gdns
Longridge rd
Nevern pl
Nevern sq
Templeton pl
Trebovir rd
Earl's Court road
Earls Court Station
Earl's Court Exhibition
West Kensington
Lanfrey pl
Mund st
Star rd
Archel rd
Chesson rd
Bramber rd
Normand Park
Lillie rd
Lillie road
North End road
Old Brompton road
West Brompton Station
Princess Beatrice Hospital
Eardley cres
Kempsford gdns
Edwardes sq
Pembroke rd
Pembroke gdns
Pembroke vlls
Pembroke sq
Logan pl
Cromwell cres
Abingdon rd
Scarsdale vi
Stratford rd
Lexham gdns
Hogarth rd
Earls Ct gdns
Barkston gdns
Hesper ms
Bramham gdns
Earl's Court
Penywern rd
Earl's Ct sq
Bolton gdns
Wetherby ms
Redcliffe close
Redcliffe sq
Coleherne rd
The Little Boltons
Phillimore gdns
Holland wlk
Sedlescombe rd
Racton rd
Anselm rd
Halford rd
Haldane rd
Tournay rd
Epirus rd
Fabian rd
Mirabel rd
Clem Atlee ct
Chestnut cl
Estcourt rd
Tamworth st
Ongar rd
Seagrave rd
Rickett st
Roxby yard
Miles
Metres
500
1000
1500

Continued on map 4

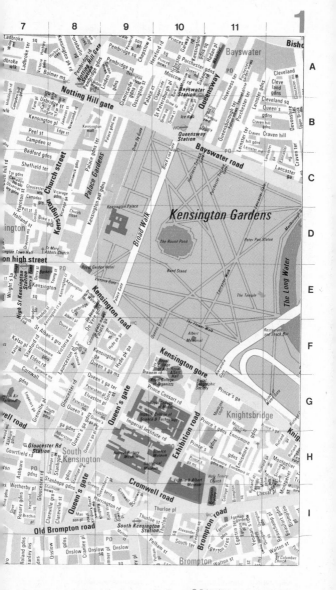

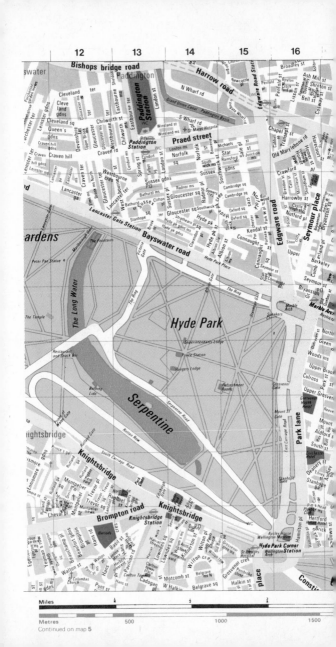

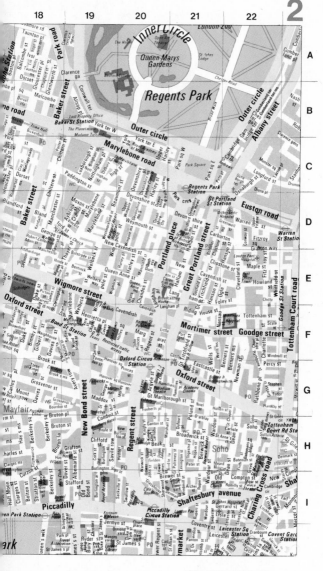

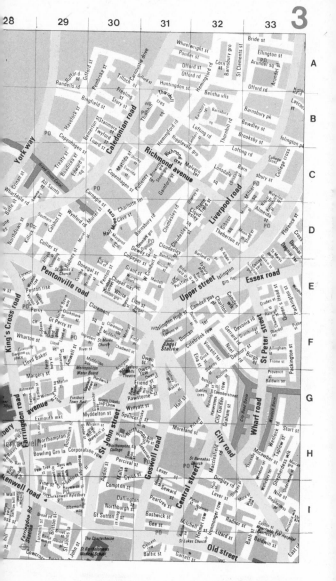

A
B
C
D
E
F
G
H
I

Wheelwright st
Ponder st
Offord st
Offord st
Cornsby gro
Barnsbury gro
St Clements st
Bride st
Ellington st
PO
Arundel sq

Ruford rd
Randells rd
Gifford st
Pentonville st
Tilloch st
Offord rd
Huntingdon st
Hemingford rd
Offord rd
Arundel pl
High st
Laycock

Bingfield st
Freeling st
Story st
Thornhill cres
Belitha vlls

York way
Havelock st
Copenhagen st
Bramton rd
Stanmore
Twyford st
Luard st
Caledonian road
Hemingford rd
Ripplevale gro
Lofting rd
Thornhill rd
Barnsbury sq
Barnsbury pk
Bewdley st
Brooksby st
Islington pk

Treaty st
Boadicea st
Edward sq
Copenhagen st
Manilla st
Richmond avenue
Richmond ter
Malvern ter
Lonsdale sq
Lofting rd
Barn
sbury st
College cross
College cross

Cynan st
All Saints
Wharfdale rd
Baltic
Southern
Calshot st
Wynford rd
Muriel
Hall
Cave st
Barnsbury gro
Cloudesley rd
Cloudesley
sq
Stonefield st
Cloud sq
Cloudesley
Liverpool road
Gibson
Theberton st
Mitford
Almeida
PO
Florence
Cross

Northdown st
Kellick st
Collier st
Caledon st
Donegal st
Romley st
Maygood st
Barnsbury st
Dewey rd
Culpeper st
Barford st
St John st
Thornhill
Cross
Dagmar
Chantrey

Lorenzo
St James's Church
Pentonville road
Penton rise
Penton st
Chapel mkt
Grant st
W Manton
Manton
Upper street
Islington grn pas
Camden pas
Essex road
Cruden st
Queen's
Passage

King's Cross road
Percy
cir
Cruikshank
Gt Percy st
Claremont
White
Lion st
Camden
Pophom st
Chantry
Devonia rd
Gerrard rd
Danbury st
Noel
Burgh
St Peter street
Pickington
Provence

Wharton st
Granville
Gwynne sq
Lloyd Baker
Margery st
River st
Myddelton
Inglebert st
Claremont
sq
Chadwell st
Owen's
Owen st
Duncan
ter
Colebrook row
Vincent ter
Frome st
Allingham st
Baldwin ter

Attneave st
Radley st
Wilmington sq
Percy
Merlin
Finsbury
Town Hall
Myddelton
Water Board
Hardwick
Sadlers Wells
Theatre
Myddelton
Friend st
Wynyatt
Half
City Garden
row
Graham st
Wenlock rd
Sturt st

Exmouth mkt
Farringdon road
avenue
Whiskin st
Rosoman
St John street
Northampton
Spencer st
Northampton sq
Wyclif
Moreland st
City road
Micawber st
Taplow st
Shepherdess wlk
Moriah

clerkenwell
Bowling Grn la
Corporation row
Northampton
College
Percival st
St Barnabas
Church
Macclesfield
Dingley rd
Nile st
Shepherdess

Pine Treet
Sans wlk
Aldgton st
Malta
Lever st
Seward
Compton st
Cyrus st
Payrol
Central street
Lever st
Radnor st
Nile st

enwell road
wall
Farringdon Rd
Turnmill st
Benja
Albion
St Johns
John
Aylebury
Northburgh st
Gt Sutton st
Dallington st
Peartree st
Bastwick st
Gee st
Mitchell
Norman
Helmet st
Lizard st
Honmonger row
Bath
Baldwin st
East

Cowcross
Britton
The Charterhouse
St Bartholomews
Medical School
Crescent
Baltic st
St Lukes Church
Garrett st
Old street

1 2 3 4 5 6

St Thomas's way

Mirabel rd
Fabian rd
Hartismere rd

Haldane rd
Anselm rd

Hacton rd

Ongar rd

Red cliffe
sq

The Little Boltons

Tournay rd
Epirus rd

Kenyon st
Armadale rd
Eustace rd

Halford rd

Westgate ter
Redcliffe gardens

Coleherne rd
Harcourt ter

Shorrolds rd

Walham gro

Mickthwaite rd

Seagrave rd

Ifield rd

Redcliffe

Tregunter rd

Dawes road

Farm la

Finborough rd

Cath
Redcliffe rd

Cathcart rd

Bishops rd

Farm la

Cath

car rd

Burnthwaite rd
Darlan rd

Jordan pl

PO

Walham Green

Faw

cett rd

Hollywood rd

Seymour rd

Redcliffe st

Elmstone rd
Harbledown rd

Poulton pl
Barclay rd

WC

Effie rd

Fulham Broadway Station

Fulham Town Hall

Chapel

Fulham road

Netherton

gro

Gertrude st
Lamont rd

Novello st
Campana rd

Cedarne rd

Harwood road

Waterford rd

Moore pk rd

Hortensia rd

St Marks Coll

Gunter gro

Edith
Slaidburn st

Edith gro

Limerston

Basuto rd
Crondace rd

Eel Brook
Common

Musgrave cres

Kempson rd

Maxwell rd

Rumbold rd

Holmead

Wandon rd

Kings road

Shalcomb st

Lamont rd

Avalon rd

Harwood ter

Edith
row

Smith
ter

Brea

Michael rd

Meek st

Lots rd
Telcott rd

Edith gro

Quarrendon rd
Chipstead
Perrymead st
Rycroft

Shalcrockhurch

Cresford

Bovingdon rd

Embden st

Upcerne
rd

Burnaby st

Ashburnham rd

Cremorne rd

Studdridge rd

Pearscroft rd

Sandilands rd

Bagley's la

Fulmead
st

Imperial rd

Uverdale
rd

Uver
Tad

Stadium st

Lots rd

Clancarty rd

Langford rd

PO

Dock

Beltran rd

Broughton rd

Elswick
st

St Marks Church

Westbridge rd

Battersea

Ashcombe
st
Harborough
st
Friston
st
Wool
neigh
st

Danbury st
Hazlebury rd
Oakbury rd
Roseberry rd

Furness rd

Stephendale rd

Elbe st

Glenrosa

Lindrop st

Peterborough rd

Townmead rd

Fulham Power Station

Vicarage cres

Kiln
pl

Gartmoor

School

Collingwoke st

Surrey

Ismailia
rd

De Morgan rd
Humble st
Althea st

Edenvale st

Quarrenden

River Thames

Granfield st

Parkham
st

Winstead

Vicarage cres

Lombard rd

Gwynne rd

Orville rd

Battersea High st

Orbel st

Holman rd
Yelverton rd

Badric rd

Winders rd

Home rd
Goulden st

Inworth rd

Simpson st

Winfield st

Edna st

Ursula st

Shuttleworth rd

Octavia st

Ballen st

Stanmer st

PO

Kambala rd

Musjid rd

Patrigoe

Sabine rd

Abercrombie st

Frere st

Mendip rd
Chatfield rd

York pl

Creek

Vernon st

Wye st

Brynmaer rd

Maysoule

Lavender

Ingrave st

Heaver rd

Mantua st

Khyber rd

Falcon st

Afghan rd

Candahar rd

Kerrison rd

Worfield st

Shilling
Tom
Long

Petergate

Usk rd

Wynter st

Hope st

Holgate st

Benham
st

Stock

Darien rd

Falcon

York road

Lavender

Plough rd

Currie
rd

Darien rd

Falcon

Miles

Metres   500   1000   1500

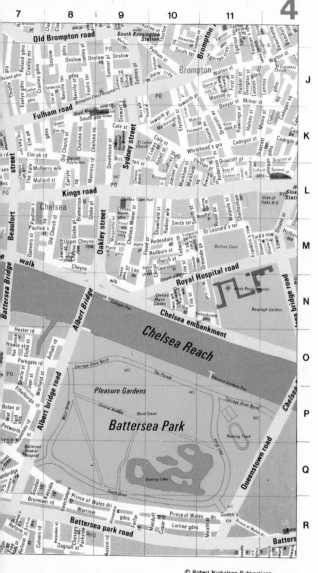

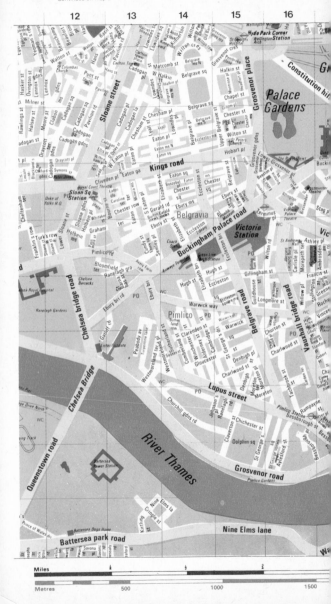

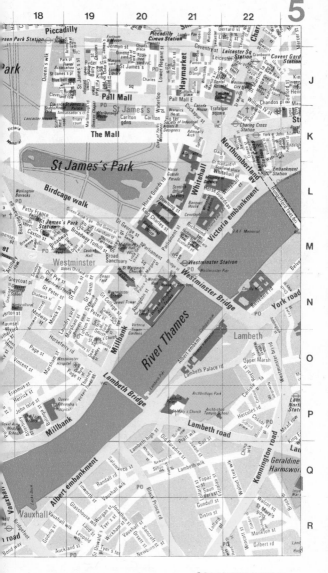

| 18 | 19 | 20 | 21 | 22 |

Green Park Station
Piccadilly
Piccadilly Circus Station
Coventry st
Leicester Sq Station
Gerrard st
London Pav
Cranbourn st
Covent Gard Station

Park
Jermyn st
Fortnum & Mason
Queen
Regent st
Haymarket
Panton st
Leicester sq
Orange st
Dental Hospital
Westminster City Sch
Kin
Hen

Queen's wlk
St James's
Ryder st
Bury st
King
St James's
sq
Charles
Lower Regent st
Pall Mall E
Canada House
Chandos pl
Mar

Pall Mall
Waterloo
Carlton
Carlton
Hotel de la Gr
Trafalgar square
Charing Cross Station
Stra

Clarence House
St James's Palace
Marlborough House
Friary court
gdns
Duke of York's
Admiralty Arch
WC
York pl
John Adam

The Mall
Admiralty
Northumberland
Embankment Station

St James's Park
Horse Guards
Horse Guards parade
Scotland place
Embankment

Wellington Barracks
Birdcage walk
Downing st
Whitehall
Horse Guards av

PO
Petty France
St James's Park Station
Old Queen st
Gt George st
King Charles st
Richmond
Banqueting House
RAF Memorial

Carton st
Broadway
Tothill st
Parliament st
Cenotaph

Westminster
Broad Sanctuary
Abbey Orchard
Deans Yd
Westminster Station
Westminster Pier

Greycoat pl
Gt Peter st
Gt Smith st
Jewel Tower
Westminster Bridge

Medway st
Marsham st
Gt College st
Abingdon st
York road

Page st
Millbank
Victoria Tower Gardens
Lambeth

Horseferry rd
PO

Vincent st
Lambeth Bridge
River Thames
Upper Marsh

Erasmus st
Herrick st
John Islip st
Queen Alexandra Hospital
Albert embankment
Lambeth Palace rd
Archbishops Park

Millbank
St Mary's Church
Archbishop Temple School
Hercules rd
Lambeth North Station

Lambeth road

Lambeth high st
Old Paradise st
Pratt wlk
Salt st
China st
Kennington road
Geraldine Harmsworth

Albert embankment
Salamanca st
Randall rd
Vauxhall wlk
Black Prince rd
Topaz
Lambeth wlk

Vauxhall
Glasshouse st
Worgan st
Jonathan st
Gunduff st
Distin st
St Mary's gdns

road
Auckland st
St Oswald's
Tyer's st
Wickham st
Oxsett st
Sancroft st
Newburn st
Monkton st
Gilbert rd

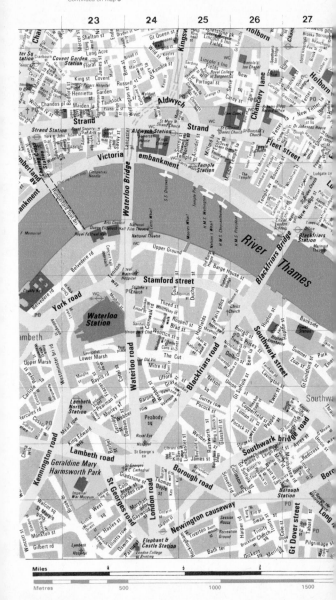

Miles		4		5		2
Metres	500			1000		1500

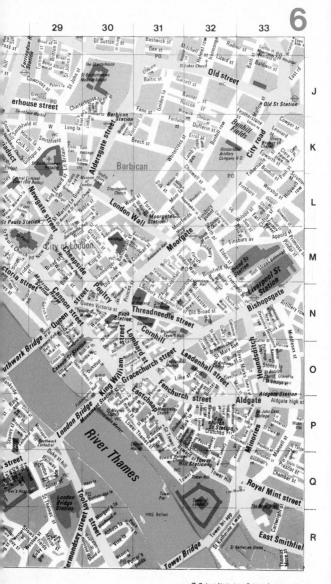

Cinemas Tel. nos.

ABC 1 & 2 836 8861
Academy 1 437 2981
Academy 2 437 5129
Academy 3 437 8819
Astral 1 & 2 437 5259
Astral 1, 2, 3 437 6359
Biograph 834 1624
Centa 437 3561 & 4 430 0631
Cinecenta 1, 2, 3 & 4 930 0631
Classic Oxford St 636 0310
Classic Leicester Sq 930 6915
Classic (Haymarket) 839 1527
Classic Cartoon 834 7641
Classic Poly 637 9963
Columbia 734 5414
Compton Cine Club 437 4555
Curzon 499 3737
Dilly Cine Club 437 6266
Dominion 580 9562
Empire 437 1234
Eros 437 3839
Essential 439 3657
Film Centa 1, 2 & 3 437 4815
Gala Royal 262 2345
Gate Two 837 1177
ICA 930 6393
Jacey 930 1143
Leicester Sq Theatre 930 5252
London Pavilion 437 2982
Metropole 437 1653
National Film Theatre 928 3232
Odeon (Haymarket) 930 2738
Odeon (Leicester Sq) 930 6111
Odeon (Marble Arch) 723 2011
Odeon Disney 836 0691
Plaza 1, 2, 3 & 4 437 1234
Prince Charles 437 8181
Ritz 437 1234
Scala 637 9309
Scene 1, 2, 3 & 4 439 4470
The Soho 734 2005
Studio 1, 2, 3 & 4 437 3300
Warner West End 439 0791

Theatres Tel. nos.

Adelphi 836 7611
Albery 836 3878
Aldwych 836 6404
Ambassadors 836 1171
Apollo 437 2663
Arts 836 2132
Astoria 734 4291
Cambridge 836 6056
Comedy 930 2578
Criterion 930 3216
Drury Lane 836 8108
Duchess 836 8243
Duke of York's 836 5122
Fortune 836 2238
Garrick 836 4601
Globe 437 1592
Haymarket 930 9832
Her Majesty's 930 6606
Jeannetta Cochrane 242 7040
Lyric 437 3686
May Fair 629 3036
National Theatre 928 2252
New London 242 9802
Old Vic 928 7616
Palace 437 6834
Palladium 437 7373
Phoenix 836 2294
Piccadilly 437 4506
Players 839 1134
Prince Edward 437 6877
Prince of Wales 930 8681
Purcell Room 928 3191
Queen Elizabeth Hall 928 3191
Queen's 734 1166
Royal Albert Hall 589 8212
Royal Festival Hall 928 3191
Royalty 405 8004
Sadler's Wells 837 1672
St Martin's 836 1443
Savoy 836 8888
Shaftesbury 836 6596
Strand 836 2660
Vaudeville 836 9988
Victoria Palace 834 1317
Warehouse 836 8608
Westminster 834 0283
Whitehall 930 6692
Wyndham's 836 3028
Young's 928 3363

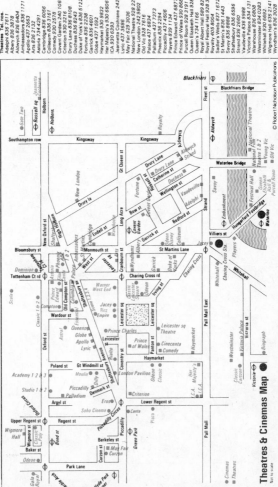

Theatres & Cinemas Map

Not to scale

● Cinemas
● Theatres

© Robert Nicholson Publications

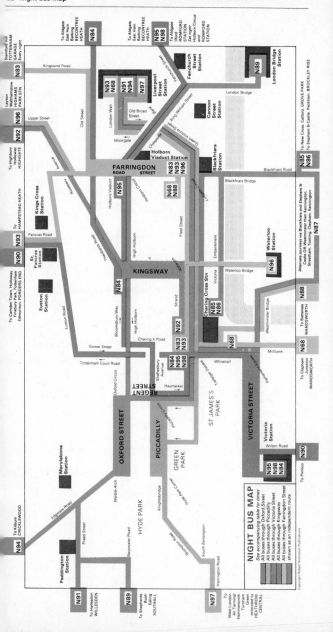

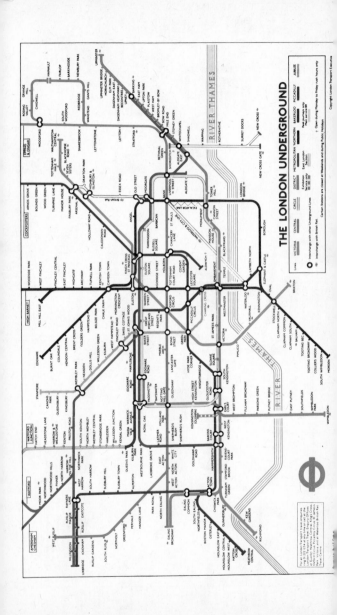

THE LONDON UNDERGROUND

RIVER THAMES

Copyright London Transport Executive